TWO OLD FOOLS IN THE KITCHEN

PART 1

SPANISH AND MIDDLE EASTERN RECIPES

TRADITIONAL AND NEW

VICTORIA TWEAD

NEW YORK TIMES BESTSELLING AUTHOR

Copyright © 2020 Victoria Twead

Cover painting, illustrations by Nick Saltmer
Photographs by Susan Franey

Formatting by Ant Press - www.antpress.org
Published by Ant Press - www.antpress.org

Available in ebook, paperback and hardback editions.

HARDBACK EDITION: ISBN: 978-1-922476-25-8

All rights reserved.

No part of this book may be reproduced in any form or by any electronic or mechanical means, including information storage and retrieval systems, without written permission from the author, except for the use of brief quotations in a book review.

A Quick Note from Victoria

Neither Joe nor I are creative, intuitive cooks. However, Joe is a skilled dishwasher-stacker, and I'm an expert recipe thief. So, when the Spanish village ladies gave me recipes, it seemed a great idea to include them in my first book, *Chickens, Mules and Two Old Fools*.

Years later, many more books have been added to the *Old Fools* series and I've continued to include recipes begged, stolen or borrowed from friends, relatives and even celebrities, like Nadia Sawalha, who generously gave me most of the Middle Eastern ones.

"Why don't you ask your Facebook friends if any of them have cooked and photographed your recipes?" asked my good friend, Hildy. "Then you'd have colour photos for the book."

"Good idea," I said, and did just that, expecting little response.

Up popped Sue Franey in England. Being stuck at home during lockdown during the Coronavirus pandemic meant she was at a loose end.

Here comes the amazing bit. Not only is Sue a lovely lady, a professional cook, but photography is her hobby!

"I'm going to try and cook every recipe in the book," she declared. "What fun!"

And she did just that.

Two Old Fools in the Kitchen was created in response to numerous requests over the years from kind readers of the *Old Fools* series who wanted to see all the recipes collected together in one place.

Sorry it's taken so long. Here you go. This is Part 1.

As I mentioned, these recipes aren't new: I stole them from the first three books of the Old Fools series:

Chickens, Mules and Two Old Fools

Two Old Fools - Olé!

Two Old Fools on a Camel

Happy cooking, and I'd really appreciate any photos of recipes you try!

Victoria Twead

For Sue Franey

Without your enthusiasm, photographs, cooking and tasting skills,
this book would not have been possible.

CONTENTS

SECTION 1
TAPAS AND SIDE DISHES

Page 10

SECTION 2
FISH, MEAT AND VEGETARIAN DISHES

Page 50

SECTION 3
DRINKS AND DESSERTS

Page 94

Acknowledgements: Page 106
About the Author: Page 106
Contacts and links: Page 106
The Old Fools series: Page 107
More books by Victoria Twead: Page 109
Preview of Chickens, Mules and Two Old Fools Page 111

RECIPES

TAPAS AND SIDE DISHES

Grumpy's Garlic Mushrooms	……………………	11
Spicy Mediterranean Dip	……………………	12
Tahini Sauce	……………………	13
Courgette Muttabal	……………………	14
Beautiful Beetroot Dip	……………………	15
Parsley Tahini Dip	……………………	16
Stuffed Tomatoes and Prawns	……………………	17
Bethina's Ham, Tomato & Garlic Toasts	……………………	18
Crispy Potatoes in Spicy Tomato Sauce	……………………	19
Sweet Potato Mash	……………………	20
Spanish Spinach	……………………	21
Spanish Potato Salad	……………………	22
Vegetable Kebabs	……………………	23
Asparagus Salad	……………………	24
Salted Almonds	……………………	25
Spanish Cauliflower and Paprika	……………………	26
Summer Baked Potatoes	……………………	27
Marinated Anchovy Tapa	……………………	28
Lebanese Minted Liver	……………………	29
Scrambled Eggs with Ham	……………………	30
Spinach and Mackerel Toasts	……………………	31
Olive Oil Infusions	……………………	32
Baked Baby Lettuce	……………………	33
Herbed Chicken Wings	……………………	34
Mediterranean Chicken Tapas	……………………	35
Roasted Chickpeas with Thyme	……………………	36
Spicy Broad Bean and Serrano Ham Fritters	……………………	37
Prawns with Garlic Mayonnaise	……………………	38
Fried Chorizo with Apple and Cider	……………………	39
Fried Chorizo in Garlic	……………………	40
Sherried Chorizo	……………………	41
Spanish Chorizo and Calamari Salad	……………………	42
Devilled Kidney and Wild Mushroom Tostada	……………………	43
Harissa: Spicy Chili Sauce	……………………	44

Hot potatoes with a White Bean and Sherry Garlic Dip	45
Jake's Dad's Thanksgiving Sweet Potato Wonderful	46
Spanish Roasted Tomatoes	47
Sambousek	48
Arabic Salad	49

FISH, MEAT AND VEGETARIAN DISHES

Barbecued Sardines	51
Tuna with a Spicy Sauce	52
Mackerel Fillets in Garlic and Paprika	53
Baked Mackerel	54
Lemon Swordfish with Roasted Tomatoes	55
Amoroso Mussels with Almonds	56
Garlic Prawns with Smoked Paprika	57
Chicken and Prawn Paella	58
Mediterranean Roast Chicken	59
Garlic and Pepper Chicken	60
Slow-Cooked Brandy Chicken	61
Honey Barbecued Chicken	62
The Gin Twins' Chuck-It-All-In Curry	63
Shish Taouk: Thyme for Kebabs	64
Mussakhan: Roast Chicken on a Magic Carpet	65
Lamb Cochifrito	66
Sheikh-al-Mahshi: Lamb-Stuffed Peppers and Aubergines	67
Barbecued Spanish Lamb	69
Spiced Lamb and Date Tagine	70
Spanish Meatballs	71
Sfeeha: Middle Eastern Lamb Mini-Pizzas	73
Shawarma: Marinated Lamb for Pita, Tortilla or Wraps	74
Beef in Fruit Sauce (Ecuadorian Recipe)	75
Marinated Spanish Beef Kebabs	76
Chickpea and Chorizo Soup	77
Summer Pork with Sherry	78
Creamy Pork and Paprika	79
Paco's Rabbit Stew	80
Warming Winter's Brunch	81
Carmen-Bethina's Poor Man's potatoes	82
Colin's Spanish Omelette	83

Gazpacho (Cold Tomato Soup) from Andalucía	……………………..	85
Roast Pumpkin with Chili and Honey	……………………..	86
Tepsi: Aubergine, Onion and Potato Bake	……………………..	87
Lentils and Oyster Mushrooms	……………………..	88
Honey, Figs and Ham	……………………..	89
True Falafels	……………………..	90
Mejeddarah: A Humble Rice and Lentil Pleasure	……………………..	91
Lentil Dream	……………………..	92
Stuff Ya Potatoes!	……………………..	93

DRINKS AND DESSERTS

Paco's Sangria	……………………..	95
The Winning Rice Pudding Recipe	……………………..	96
Sticky Toffee Pudding a la Glennys	……………………..	97
Mama Ufarte's Lemony Sponge	……………………..	99
Cousin Elias's Easy Peasy Carrot Cake	……………………..	100
Three Kings Cake	……………………..	101
The FNJ (Figgy-Nutty-Jammy) Brioche	……………………..	102
Baklava	……………………..	103
Rosewater and Pistachio Ice-cream	……………………..	105

SECTION 1

TAPAS AND SIDE DISHES

Tapa means 'lid' or 'cover' in Spanish. It's thought that the name originally came from the practice of placing slices of meat on top of a sherry glass, to keep out flies.

The meat, often ham or chorizo, was characteristically salty, inducing thirst. Bartenders saw this and began serving a variety of tapas which increased alcohol sales.

Thus a new tradition was born.

GRUMPY'S GARLIC MUSHROOMS
Champiñones al Ajillo

TAPAS
VEGETARIAN
EASY

Hard to photograph but oh, so simple to cook and eat, this is the most bookmarked recipe in the collection.

Ingredients (serves 4)

50ml (2 fl oz) extra virgin olive oil

250g (8 oz) fresh mushrooms (sliced)

4 - 6 cloves of garlic (chopped or sliced)

3 tablespoons dry Spanish sherry

2 tablespoons lemon juice

Large pinch of dried chili flakes

Large pinch of paprika

Salt, freshly ground pepper

Chopped parsley to garnish

Method

- Heat the oil in a frying pan and fry the mushrooms over a high heat for 2 or 3 minutes. Stir constantly.
- Lower the heat and add the garlic, lemon juice, sherry, salt and pepper.
- For a milder flavour you can leave it at that if you like. But if you like a few 'fireworks', now is the time to add the dried chili and paprika as well.
- Cook for another 5 minutes or so until the garlic and mushrooms have softened, then remove from the heat.
- Sprinkle with chopped parsley and divide up into pre-heated little dishes.
- Serve with plenty of fresh, crusty bread to mop up the seriously garlicky juices.

> *Grumpy, the bartender, wiped his hands on his apron and approached our table, flicking off imaginary crumbs from the plastic tablecloth with the back of his hand. He had a splendid moustache which concealed any expression he may have had, and made communication difficult.*
>
> *"Could we see the menu, please?" asked Joe in his best phrase book Spanish.*
>
> *Grumpy shook his head and snorted. It seemed there was no menu.*
>
> *From Chickens, Mules and Two Old Fools*

SPICY MEDITERRANEAN DIP

TAPAS
VEGETARIAN
FAIRLY EASY

A mildly spicy, smooth, light dip perfect for an aperitif or buffet.

Ingredients

1 large jar of chickpeas (not dried)
175 ml (6 fl oz) olive oil
Salt
1 teaspoon pepper
2 tablespoons cumin
2 teaspoons hot paprika

Method

- Place the chickpeas and the olive oil into a large bowl and blend into a smooth puree.
- Add the salt and pepper and the cumin and blend again. It's important to taste as you go, adding more cumin as necessary.
- Pour into a dish, sprinkling the top with a little more cumin and the hot paprika.
- Place in the freezer for about 10 minutes to set slightly.
- Serve with slices of raw carrot, cucumber, peppers and celery.

❝The sofa was abandoned in the middle of the road. Joe was frog-marched back down the street while Bethina and I followed, my arm clamped in a vice-like grip.

Just before we reached our house, they stopped and pushed open the front door beside ours. It became clear that these were our next door neighbours, and we were herded into their little house. What a contrast! Where our house was dusty and damp, their house smelled of herbs and the white walls gleamed. Framed family photographs hung in neat rows and a vase of wild flowers stood on the table.

"You will have something to eat and drink, no?" said Paco and pressed us into chairs.❞

From *Chickens, Mules and Two Old Fools*

TAHINI SAUCE
The serve-with-everything sauce

VEGETARIAN
FAIRLY EASY

This sauce is extremely versatile, and can be served with fish, any grilled meat or, if thinned down a little more, as a salad dressing.

Ingredients (serves 4 - 6)

4 tbsp tahini (from most big stores and online)
3 tbsp lemon juice
Salt
2 - 6 tbsp warm water

Method

- Place the tahini, lemon juice and salt
- in a small bowl.
- Gradually add the water whilst whisking.
- (You may need more water if it's sticky.)
- It's ready to use when it has the consistency of double cream.

According to Wikipedia, tahini is made from sesame seeds that are soaked in water and then crushed to separate the bran from the kernels. The crushed seeds are soaked in salt water, causing the bran to sink. The floating kernels are skimmed off the surface, toasted, and ground to produce an oily paste.

COURGETTE MUTTABAL
Simple Summertime Dip

TAPAS
VEGETARIAN
FAIRLY EASY

"This is an easy but deliciously summery dip," says Nadia Sawalha. "It goes beautifully alongside any plain meat or fish."

Ingredients (serves 6 as part of a meze)

450g (1lb) courgettes (pale green ones if possible)

Olive oil

2 large garlic cloves, peeled

Salt

Juice of 1 or 2 lemons

4 - 6 tbsp tahini, loosened with a little warm water

Method

- Peel the courgettes and cut them into thick slices.
- Heat a generous tbsp of oil with a few tbsp water in a pan and steam-fry the courgettes in the covered pan until soft.
- With a pestle and mortar, pound the garlic and courgettes with 2 tsp of salt until smooth.
- When ready to serve, stir in most of the lemon juice, then gradually add the tahini.
- Beat well and adjust the flavour with more lemon juice, salt and a good slosh of oil.
- Garnish with spices/herbs of your own choice. Mint, pomegranate seeds, sumac, experiment!
- Serve with warmed pita bread.

BEAUTIFUL BEETROOT DIP

TAPAS
VEGETARIAN
FAIRLY EASY

When the purple of the beetroot is puréed with the tahini and lemon juice, this dip is transformed into an almost neon pink. Try this with white fish, chicken or even in a cheese sandwich.

Ingredients (serves 6 - 8)

3 large beetroot, cooked
1 tsp salt
2 garlic cloves, peeled and crushed (optional)
60ml (2 fl oz) lemon juice
125ml (4 fl oz) tahini
55ml (2 fl oz) warm water

Method

- Mash the beetroot to a purée, or leave a bit more texture (your choice).
- In a separate bowl, add the salt, garlic, lemon juice, tahini and water.
- Mix until smooth and creamy.
- Add more water if the tahini becomes sticky, and keep stirring.
- Stir in the beetroot.
- Serve with warm pita bread, or crisp Cos lettuce leaves, to dip and scoop.

PARSLEY TAHINI DIP

> TAPAS
> VEGETARIAN
> FAIRLY EASY

"This is such a fabulously versatile summer dip that I beg you to try it," says Nadia Sawalha. "It is the perfect partner for barbecued or grilled fish, lamb or chicken. And, for all vegans, it's ideal when poured over steamed vegetables or dipped into with a hunk of hot pita bread."

Ingredients (serves 6)

1 tsp salt (exercise your taste buds!)

1 - 2 garlic cloves, peeled and roughly chopped

300ml (½ pint) white tahini (the wholefood one won't do!)

Juice of 2 lemons (taste and decide!)

Warm water to thin

Very large handful of fresh, finely chopped parsley

Method

- Pound the garlic and salt with a pestle and mortar until really smooth.
- Add the tahini and mix with a whisk.
- Add the lemon juice and keep whisking.
- When it looks really strange and sticky, add the warm water, whisking all the time.
- Finally, stir in the green parsley.

STUFFED TOMATOES AND PRAWNS

TAPAS
SEAFOOD
FAIRLY EASY

Stuffed tomatoes are a classic tapas dish and bring colour to the tapas table. A very simple combination stuffed with heaps of Mediterranean flavour.

Ingredients (makes 4 tapas)

200g (8 oz) large cooked prawns
4 olives
4 large vine ripened tomatoes
1 stick celery
2 tablespoons mayonnaise
2 mint leaves
Parsley

Method

- Roughly chop the prawns and mint leaves, thinly slice the celery, then mix with the mayonnaise.
- Cut the tops off the tomatoes and carefully remove the insides (a melon baller works well).
- Place 1 olive in the bottom of each tomato, then stuff with the prawn mix.
- Drizzle with olive oil and garnish with parsley.

" Carmen-Bethina popped round to give us a bag of tomatoes from her son Diego's greenhouse empire. "

From *Two Old Fools - Olé!*

BETHINA'S HAM, TOMATO AND GARLIC TOASTS
Jamón, Tomate y Ajo con Pan

TAPAS
MEAT
EASY

Perfect as a breakfast, lunch or late night snack.

Ingredients

Slices of bread (baguette, cut diagonally)
1 clove garlic, cut in half
1 very ripe tomato
Slices of jamon serrano or ham of your choice
Extra virgin olive oil

Method

Preheat the grill.
Toast the bread and, while still warm, rub with the halved garlic to flavour the slices.
Rub the bread with the halved tomato. Squeeze in as much of the flesh as you can.
Sprinkle with a pinch of salt and freshly-ground pepper.
Drizzle with some extra virgin olive oil and top it off with the ham.

> "Women!" said Paco, putting his arm round Joe's shoulders. "What do they know about good wine?"
>
> Bethina clattered around her tiny kitchen while the red wine flowed freely. She put plates of smoked ham, tomato, cheese and bread on the plastic tablecloth then joined us to sit at the table. A goodly amount of her body spilled over the edges of her chair.

From Chickens, Mules and Two Old Fools

"We absolutely loved this. Could be a regular to have with our evening beer/cider."

Sue Franey, chef and photographer of the Old Fools' recipes

CRISPY POTATOES IN SPICY TOMATO SAUCE
Patatas Bravas

TAPAS
VEGETARIAN
SOME SKILL

Nobody can resist this classic tapas dish. Wonderful chunks of potato in a spicy tomato sauce.

Ingredients (serves 4)

1 kg (2lb) potatoes, peeled, and cut into 2cm (1in) inch cubes
1 small onion, finely chopped
2 cloves garlic, crushed
Salt and freshly ground black pepper
500g (1lb) tomatoes
3 teaspoons (paprika
¼ teaspoon cayenne pepper
¼ teaspoon chopped fresh thyme
1 teaspoon tomato puree
Olive oil, for frying
Chopped parsley to garnish

Method

- Par-boil the potatoes for 5 to 10 minutes. Drain the water.
- Let the steam evaporate for a minute or so and then give the pan a good shake. This roughs up the outsides nicely. Set aside.
- Prepare the tomatoes by cutting a cross in the base and plunging them into boiling water for 10 to 15 seconds. Plunge into cold water and the skin should peel away easily. Chop the tomatoes.
- Fry the onion until soft. Add the garlic, paprika, thyme and cayenne pepper, then cook for another couple of minutes.
- Add the chopped tomato and puree and cook, uncovered, until the sauce thickens, about 20 minutes.
- During cooking, add the salt and pepper to taste. If the sauce seems too dry, add a little water.
- Meanwhile, re-heat the frying oil and fry the potatoes until golden brown. This gives them a crisp coating and prevents the sauce from soaking in too much. They should be beautifully crisp outside and soft and fluffy inside.
- To serve, place the potatoes in a serving bowl, then cover with the spicy sauce.
- Sprinkle with chopped parsley.

SWEET POTATO MASH

**TAPAS
VEGETARIAN
FAIRLY EASY**

This rich, creamy potato dish is a lovely vegetarian dish and also a really nice accompaniment to roasted meats.

Ingredients

1 large orange sweet potato

3 potatoes

25g (1 oz) butter

125ml (4 fl oz) cream

Olive oil

Nutmeg, grated

100g (3 - 4 oz) cheese, grated

Method

- Rub the sweet potato with a little olive oil and bake in a medium oven for 25 minutes until cooked.
- Peel and wash the potatoes. Cook in a pan of salted boiling water until tender, drain and mash well and place into a large bowl or pan.
- Remove the sweet potato from the oven and scoop out the flesh.
- Mix with the mashed potato, add the butter and cream and beat well together. It should now almost resemble a smooth purée.
- Season with salt and pepper, and then transfer to a gratin or shallow dish. Sprinkle with grated cheese and dust with a little nutmeg.
- Place under the grill until the cheese begins to bubble, and serve.

" We explained that delivery vans came almost daily with bread, fish and local produce, and that the doctor came once a week and held a surgery in one of the villager's living rooms. Anna looked dubious. "

From *Two Old Fools - Ole!*

SPANISH SPINACH
Espinacas a la España

TAPAS
VEGETARIAN
FAIRLY EASY

A very simple, tasty side dish. A sprinkling of crumbled blue cheese or feta is a delicious variation.

Ingredients (serves 2 as a side dish)

500g (18 oz) fresh spinach leaves
4 cloves garlic
Extra virgin olive oil
Salt

Method

- Trim the stems of the spinach and wash the leaves by rinsing under running water to remove any dirt.
- Drain the spinach and pat the leaves dry with kitchen paper.
- Peel and slice the garlic and then heat the oil in a large frying pan.
- Add the sliced garlic and sauté for a few minutes until it begins to brown.
- Add the spinach to the pan, pressing down with your hand to get it all in, then turn the spinach a few times to coat it all with garlic and olive oil.
- Cover and reduce the heat and cook for a minute or so.
- Turn the spinach over and cook for another minute until the spinach is nicely wilted.
- Drain any excess liquid and serve immediately with an extra drizzle of olive oil and a little salt to season.

❝ *We explained that delivery vans came almost daily with bread, fish and local produce, and that the doctor came once a week and held a surgery in one of the villager's living rooms. Anna looked dubious.* ❞

From *Chickens, Mules and Two Old Fools*

SPANISH POTATO SALAD

TAPAS
VEGETARIAN
SOME SKILL

Spanish potato salad is a popular tapa dish that goes particularly well with beer, so highly recommended at a barbecue.

Ingredients

3 medium potatoes
150g (5 oz) fresh or frozen peas
120g (4 oz) green beans
1 large carrot
1 small onion
1 small red pepper
2 tablespoons green olives
2 hard boiled eggs
1 medium tomato
1 tablespoon capers

The Dressing

200ml (7 fl oz) mayonnaise
1 teaspoon French mustard
1 tablespoon lemon juice

Method

- Peel and dice the carrot and potato. Boil the potato and carrot in water until just tender.
- Add the peas and green beans and cook for a further 5 minutes until all the vegetables are cooked.
- Drain and place in a large bowl or serving dish.
- Peel and finely chop the onion, chop the pepper and tomato and slice the hard boiled eggs.
- Add the pepper, onion, eggs, capers, tomato and olives to the other vegetables and mix together.
- In a separate bowl, make the dressing by mixing together the mayonnaise, mustard and lemon juice.
- Slowly spoon the dressing onto the salad and mix together without smothering the salad.
- Garnish with chopped parsley and freshly ground black pepper.

> *The food was always fresh, heavily laced with garlic but very strange to our British palates. Once we were served little roast birds not much bigger than sparrows. They lay upside down on our plates with their tiny feet in the air.*
>
> From *Chickens, Mules and Two Old Fools*

VEGETABLE KEBABS
Brochetas de Verduras

**TAPAS
VEGETARIAN
EASY**

These easy-to-make vegetable kebabs are a great accompaniment to any barbecue. Use any combination of your favourite vegetables, these ingredients are just suggestions.

Ingredients (serves 4)

1 aubergine
8 - 10 cherry tomatoes
1 medium red pepper
1 medium green pepper
1 medium onion
8 - 10 mushrooms
Fresh or dried thyme
Olive oil

Method

- Cut all vegetables into bite sized slices.
- Peel the onion and slice.
- Create the kebabs by alternating.
- Pour a generous amount of olive oil into a large shallow dish, adding plenty of thyme.
- Lay the kebabs in the oil and allow to marinade for about 2 hours. Turn occasionally.
- Add the kebabs and allow to marinade in the oil turning now and then for an hour or so.
- Cook on a barbecue or grill until ready.
- Serve with barbecued meat and crusty bread.

> *Provisions arrived daily in small white vans which wended their way down into the valley. They announced their arrival to the villagers by hooting furiously during their entire descent into the valley, ceasing only when they reached the square. Bethina, starched apron crackling, marched me along to introduce me to the delights of buying from the back of these vans. Bread, fish, vegetables and fruit, all fresh, all local. On Sundays, delicious cakes came with the bread.*
>
> From *Chickens, Mules and Two Old Fools*

ASPARAGUS SALAD
Ensalada de Espárragos

TAPAS
VEGETARIAN
EASY

This is the basic Spanish recipe, but you could add different ingredients such as cucumber, red or yellow pepper, olives or apple.

Ingredients

150g (6 oz) fresh green asparagus

2 medium tomatoes

2 medium potatoes

50g (2 oz) sweet corn

Olive oil

Salt and pepper to season

Method

- Boil the potatoes for about 8 minutes until cooked but still firm, drain and allow to cool.
- Trim the ends of the asparagus, removing any hard bits then blanch in boiling water for a few minutes until just tender, drain and allow to cool.
- When cool, peel the potatoes and cut into bite sized pieces, then cut the tomatoes into similar sized chunks.
- Arrange the potatoes, tomatoes, sweet corn and asparagus onto a serving dish, drizzle with olive oil and then season.

> The abandoned table looked as though a plague of soldier ants had marched through. Bethina, best apron flapping, assisted by Sofía and various female relations, cleared it all up, then dumped more plates of food on the table.
>
> From *Chickens, Mules and Two Old Fools*

SALTED ALMONDS
Almendras

TAPAS
VEGETARIAN
FAIRLY EASY

Carmen-Bethina often fried almonds in a frying pan with olive oil over an open flame. She then sprinkled them with salt and served them as nibbles to accompany Paco's wine.

Ingredients

4 cups blanched almonds
1 tbsp coarse sea salt
1 tsp paprika
2 tbsp extra virgin olive oil

Method

- Blanch the almonds by pouring boiling water over. Allow them to stand for 1 minute.
- Drain and dry with paper towels. The skins will now rub off easily.
- Grind the sea salt and paprika using a pestle and mortar. Mix well together.
- Preheat the oven to 180C (350F).
- Spread the almonds evenly on a baking sheet making sure they don't touch each other.
- Toast for 8 - 10 minutes or until golden brown.
- Transfer almonds to a bowl and drizzle enough oil over to coat evenly.
- Add the paprika and salt mixture. Toss thoroughly and serve.

❝Often, when we visited Marcia and Old Sancho's shop, we were given presents. Marcia would hand us a plastic carrier bag containing almonds, tomatoes, peppers or melons. Sometimes she presented us with a plate of rice pudding. On Old Sancho's eighty-third birthday we were given slices of cake.❞
From *Chickens, Mules and Two Old Fools*

SPANISH CAULIFLOWER AND PAPRIKA
Ajoarriero

TAPAS
VEGETARIAN
FAIRLY EASY

Serve as a vegetable accompaniment or in smaller portions as a tapas dish. Goes well with a full-bodied red wine.

Ingredients

1 large cauliflower, washed and broken into florets

6 cloves garlic

Handful fresh parsley, roughly chopped

3 tablespoons olive oil (plus extra for frying)

2 teaspoons sweet smoked paprika (or hot paprika for more bite)

Splash white wine vinegar

1 teaspoon sea salt

Method

- Cook the cauliflower in salted boiling water for 8 minutes or so until just tender.
- Drain, reserving a little of the water and set aside in a serving dish to keep warm.
- Meanwhile peel the garlic and crush 3 of the cloves, slicing the other three.
- In a small bowl or mortar, mix together the three crushed cloves of garlic with the parsley and the salt and stir in the olive oil.
- In a frying pan, heat a little olive oil and sauté the three sliced cloves of garlic until they begin to turn gently golden.
- Turn down the heat and add the contents of the mortar.
- Add the reserved cooking water from the cauliflower, paprika and a splash of wine vinegar.
- Turn up the heat and bring to the boil, cooking for a couple of minutes.
- Pour the sauce over the cauliflower in the serving dish and serve straight away.

> "What did you mean about the cauliflower?"
>
> "That's his name, dear. Cauliflower. He's a Brit, and Mother says he's always been called that, though most people call him 'Caul' for short."

From *Chickens, Mules and Two Old Fools*

SUMMER BAKED POTATOES
Patata de Verano

**TAPAS
VEGETARIAN
EASY**

These baked potatoes are great cooked on the barbecue and are full of Mediterranean flavours.

Ingredients

4 medium sized potatoes
4 cloves garlic
Oregano
Thyme
Salt
Olive oil

Method

- Wash the potatoes and cut in half, lengthways.
- Peel and crush the garlic and roughly chop the thyme and oregano (dried herbs are also good here).
- On one half of each potato, generously sprinkle the garlic and herbs, add a pinch of salt and a small drizzle of olive oil.
- Put the remaining half of the potato back on top, wrap in foil and cook in the BBQ embers for about 40 minutes, depending on size.
- You can also cook the potatoes in the oven.

> *Joe had to stoop frequently as the doorways were built for people much shorter than ourselves. Dried hams and rusty agricultural tools hung from the ceilings. Sacks of potatoes leaned against crumbling walls.*
>
> *The only bathroom was downstairs. It boasted a miniature green bath complete with plastic curtain and a chipped sink propped up at a crazy angle by bits of wood.*

From *Chickens, Mules and Two Old Fools*

MARINATED ANCHOVY TAPA
Tapa de Anchoas

TAPAS
SEAFOOD
SOME SKILL

Bought fresh, these appetising little fish can be cleaned and marinated in sherry vinegar with garlic and olive oil. They are so small they don't need cooking and are a real favourite in the summer months.

Ingredients

8 - 10 fresh anchovies
150ml (5 fl oz) sherry vinegar
Juice 1 lemon
1 garlic clove (crushed)
Handful broadleaf parsley
100ml (3½ fl oz) extra virgin olive oil

Method

- Remove the heads from the fish, split down the middle, remove the spine and rinse the fillets.
- Lay the fillets skin side up in a dish and pour sherry vinegar over, after 20 minutes the fish will turn pale.
- Remove the fish from the vinegar and place into another dish. Mix up the remaining ingredients and add to the fish.
- Marinade in the fridge for 1 - 2 hours, then serve on crusty bread.

"Really enjoying sitting on the roof terrace, but I think there are even more Spanish flies than Aussie ones! How do you put up with them?

Getting the hang of the bread, fruit and fish vans that come to the village now. Bit different to our shopping malls back home!"

Cheers from
Glennys and Ken

From *Chickens, Mules and Two Old Fools*

LEBANESE MINTED LIVER

TAPAS
MEAT
SOME SKILL

Nadia Sawalha says, "If you don't fancy liver and hummus, try this Lebanese recipe, which is so easy to make and has a really unique flavour. The original doesn't use wine, and if you prefer, you can replace it with vinegar. Be really careful not to overcook the liver, because it will absolutely ruin the dish."

Ingredients (serves 4 - 6)

450g (1lb) liver, sliced (calf's or your choice)
Salt and black pepper
2 tsp olive oil
25g (1 oz) butter
1 onion, peeled and thinly sliced
2 garlic cloves, peeled and chopped
125ml (4 fl oz) white wine or white wine vinegar
1½ tsp plain flour
1 tbsp dried mint, crushed
3 - 4 tbsp cold water
Fresh coriander, chopped

Method

- Season the liver with salt and black pepper.
- Heat the oil in a heavy-based frying pan, then drop in most of the butter.
- Once melted, flash-fry the liver on both sides. Remove from the pan and set aside.
- Add a little more butter if it needs it, then fry the garlic and onion until soft.
- Now pour in the wine and let the alcohol burn off a little.
- Add the flour and stir for a minute or so, then add the mint and water, letting it bubble for a few minutes.
- Add the liver to the sauce, and, if necessary, add a little more water.
- Allow to simmer for a few minutes until the liver is just cooked.
- Pierce with a sharp knife to check whether it is cooked through.
- Sprinkle with a little freshly chopped coriander and serve.

SCRAMBLED EGGS WITH HAM
Huevos Revueltos con Jamón

TAPAS
MEAT
EASY

Scrambled eggs are a traditional tapa in Spain. This recipe uses serrano ham but you can use all kinds of ingredients. Try it with bacon, chorizo, asparagus, mushrooms or onions.

Ingredients

50g (2 oz) jamón serrano or other ham

1 tbsp olive oil (for frying)

4 eggs

2 tbsp milk (optional)

salt and pepper

Method

- Cut the jamón into small pieces.
- Beat the eggs together with the milk (if desired) and season with salt and pepper.
- Stir in the chopped jamón and pour into a frying pan. As the egg is cooking, gently stir it until it is cooked through but still very soft. Keep a close eye on it, if you leave it too long it will go like rubber...
- Once it's ready, get it on your plate straight away and serve with crusty bread. Tapas recipes don't come much simpler than this!

> *Joe took a dozen eggs with him to Marcia's shop to give away. It was the weekend and the bread van happened to be there surrounded by village ladies.*
>
> *"Would anyone like some eggs?" he asked.*
>
> *He was almost trampled in the rush. The eggs were snatched out of his hands, and orders were placed for more. One of the Smart Ladies advised Joe to charge 70 cents for half a dozen in future, and so our unplanned business was born.*
>
> From *Chickens, Mules and Two Old Fools*

Oh, scrambled eggs with Serrano ham, what a great breakfast!

Sue Franey, chef and photographer of the Old Fools' recipes

SPINACH AND MACKEREL TOASTS

TAPAS
FISH
FAIRLY EASY

A lovely, colourful, slightly unusual, tasty dish for summer days. Great for an aperitif, buffet, tapas party dish, or whatever takes your fancy.

Ingredients (makes about 10)

2 small tins mackerel fillets in olive oil

1 french style baguette cut into rounds
(make the cut diagonally to get bigger rounds)

Bunch fresh spinach

2 cloves garlic

Method

- Wash and drain the spinach, peel and finely chop the garlic.
- Drain the oil from the mackerel, place onto a plate and roughly break up the fillets with a fork.
- Heat a little olive oil in a pan and gently cook the garlic until it begins to soften.
- Add the spinach and cook covered for a minute or so.
- Turn the spinach over to get a good coating of oil, put the lid back on and cook for a further minute.
- Remove from the pan and drain away any excess liquid.
- Toast the bread lightly on each side and arrange onto a large plate.
- Place a small amount of spinach onto each piece of toast and then top with the mackerel.

" There was just too much choice. The display was a work of art, fish of every shape and hue reposing on beds of ice. "

From *Chickens, Mules and Two Old Fools*

OLIVE OIL INFUSIONS

VEGETARIAN

EASY

Flavoured olive oils are a favourite in Andalucía. Add extra flavour and aroma to a bottle of olive oil by simply adding a few ingredients and letting them infuse together. Easy to make and the longer you keep, it the more intense the flavour.

Method

Simply add any of the following ingredients to the olive oil. You can add the ingredients on their own or combine them how you like.

Choose from:

- whole peeled cloves of garlic
- sprigs of thyme
- sprigs of rosemary
- whole black peppercorns
- dried chili peppers

Once the oil has been allowed to rest and infuse (for at least a week), use it to drizzle over salads or pizzas, spice up pasta or simply serve with crusty bread for a true Spanish delight.

In autumn, the olives and almonds were harvested. Nets were spread under the trees and families knocked the branches with sticks to dislodge the fruit and nuts.

From *Two Old Fools - Olé!*

BAKED BABY LETTUCE

TAPAS
VEGETARIAN
EASY

This slightly unusual dish is a great side dish or starter.

Ingredients

4 baby lettuces such as Little Gem
Half litre (17 fl oz) chicken or vegetable stock
2 tablespoons extra virgin olive oil
Few sprigs fresh thyme
Few sprigs fresh rosemary
Salt and pepper

Method

- Wash the lettuces, trim off the ends and remove any brown outer leaves.
- Place the lettuces in an oven dish or earthenware cazuela and pour the stock over.
- Drizzle the oil over, then pull the needles off the rosemary sprigs and the leaves off the thyme sprigs. Sprinkle over the lettuces, and season with salt and pepper.
- Cover with foil or a lid and cook for 20 to 25 minutes until the lettuces are soft and tender.

> "I wish you would walk," I said crossly to Snap-On who seemed to get heavier every second. Balancing him, the bucket and spade, the tennis racquet and the walking stick wasn't easy. I glanced across at the little patch of cultivated land where Uncle Felix grew neat lines of baby lettuce. The new green leaves contrasted vividly against the freshly watered black soil.

From *Two Old Fools - Olé!*

Baked 'baby' lettuce! I'm afraid they are not so baby at the moment, though, as our veg garden is overflowing with salad leaves, but delicious all the same. I served it with my homemade bread. (See photo)

Linda Powdrill, reader and Facebook friend

HERBED CHICKEN WINGS

TAPAS
MEAT
FAIRLY EASY

This dish is simple and tasty and makes for great summer tapas, a must at any summer function.

Ingredients (tapas for 4)

12 chicken wings, tips removed and cut in half at the joint

3 cloves garlic

Bunch fresh parsley

2 teaspoons dried oregano

Large sprig fresh thyme

Half teaspoon ground black pepper

Salt

Glass dry white wine

Juice of half a lemon

100ml (3.5 fl oz) olive oil

Method

- Peel and crush the garlic, finely chop the parsley and thyme.
- Mix all of the ingredients except the chicken in a bowl and leave to infuse for half an hour or so.
- Place the prepared chicken wings in a resealable freezer bag and add the other ingredients. Close the bag and knead well or shake the bag up to ensure a good covering.
- Leave in the fridge to marinate for two hours or so, shaking the bag from time to time.
- Place the wings onto a greased oven tray, pouring over any leftover marinade, and cook in a hot oven for 20 to 30 minutes, turning halfway until golden brown and beginning to crisp.

There is a pretty cascading waterfall and so much spring water in the area that huge pipes channel it away. Some goes to fill the town swimming pool and the rest is destined for other needs, such as irrigating the vast orange and lemon orchards, a feature of the area.

From *Two Old Fools - Olé!*

MEDITERRANEAN CHICKEN TAPAS

TAPAS
MEAT
EASY

Homemade mini chicken bites Mediterranean style, with hints of garlic and lemon, perfect for outdoor summer evenings.

Ingredients

2 chicken breasts
4 cloves garlic
Juice of 2 lemons
4 tablespoons olive oil
Flour for coating

Method

- Cut the chicken breasts into bite-sized pieces.
- Place the chicken into a bowl, add the olive oil, the juice of two lemons and the garlic, peeled and crushed.
- Leave to marinate for 2 to 3 hours in the fridge.
- Once marinated, roll the chicken pieces in the flour.
- Shake off the excess and fry in hot olive oil for about 15 to 20 minutes until golden brown and tender.
- Sprinkle with a little salt, serve with alioli (garlic mayonnaise) or tomato salsa.

> We had watched her grow from sickly puppy to barrel-on-legs and it was easy to see why. Bianca had become the family dustbin. All Carmen-Bethina's cooking scraps and left-over dinners were disposed of inside Bianca. Brown eyes innocent, tongue lolling, she had also become a master thief. Turn one's back on anything vaguely edible, and Bianca snaffled it.

From *Two Old Fools - Olé!*

ROASTED CHICKPEAS WITH THYME

TAPAS
VEGETARIAN
EASY

Chickpeas, or garbanzos, are a regular ingredient in many Spanish recipes, usually served with lamb, pork or as a side dish. One alternative way of cooking chickpeas is to roast them in the oven. Serve them up in small tapas bowls as a change from peanuts. Tremendously healthy and full of flavour, chickpeas make ideal and unusual tapas at any time.

Ingredients

Chickpeas, soaked or cooked
Sea salt
Dried thyme (or herbs of choice)
Olive oil

Method

- Preheat the oven to 180°C (355°F).
- Drain and dry the chickpeas.
- Place the chickpeas in a bowl and drizzle with olive oil before giving them a good mix by hand, making sure they are covered in oil.
- Place on a baking tray, sprinkle with salt and roast in the oven for 25 minutes, giving them a shake halfway through.
- Remove from the oven and season well with your chosen herbs (smoked paprika also works well).
- Serve hot or cold.

❝ *The Log Man reversed awkwardly down the narrow street and parked with a hiss of air-brakes. He let down the side of the truck and stood aside to allow his young helper to climb up and hurl all the logs into the street. All shapes and sizes, the logs piled up into a jumbled, precarious heap of olive wood, almond, fig, some great stumps, ragged timber wedges and perfectly round logs that bounced and rolled.* ❞

From *Two Old Fools - Olé!*

SPICY BROAD BEAN AND SERRANO HAM FRITTERS

TAPAS
MEAT
EASY

If you like your Spanish tapas hot and spicy, then this Serrano ham and broad bean recipe will certainly get the taste buds tingling. Serrano ham and broad beans are enjoyed together in tapas bars all over Spain. In certain bars you can see the locals shelling the beans and dipping them in a little salt before accompanying them with a wafer-thin slice of ham, washed down with a glass of ice-cold Fino sherry.

For this recipe these simple fritters combine the same flavour combination but with the added kick of chili and a hint of hot smoked paprika.

Ingredients

250g (9 oz) fresh broad beans
100g (3 - 4 oz) diced Serrano ham
A quarter teaspoon hot smoked paprika
1 small red chili pepper (diced)
1 tablespoon plain flour
Half a lemon
Salt
Olive oil
Cracked black pepper

Method

- Shell the broad beans and place into a food processor.
- Add the diced ham along with the smoked paprika and chili pepper.
- Squeeze the juice of half the lemon into the mix.
- Blend for a few seconds until the ingredients become the texture of breadcrumbs.
- Remove the mixture and tip into a bowl.
- Season with salt and pepper and add the flour, mixing together using a fork.
- Meanwhile, heat a good inch (3 cm) of olive oil in a frying pan.
- Using two tablespoons, shape your fritters by rolling between the two and add to the oil, fry until deep golden brown on the outside.
- Serve with a cool yogurt mint dip.

Sue Franey, chef and photographer of the Old Fools' recipes

I didn't think we'd like these but we were surprised. They turned out to be really tasty!

PRAWNS WITH GARLIC MAYONNAISE

**TAPAS
SEAFOOD
EASY**

A common Christmas meal starter. Use shelled, frozen prawns if you prefer, although fresh ones are more flavoursome.

Ingredients

50g (2 oz) mayonnaise

50g (2 oz) large prawns

1 large clove of garlic, crushed

Sea salt

Method

- Mix the mayonnaise and crushed garlic in a bowl and set aside.
- Shell the prawns and place on a baking tray.
- Sprinkle with a little sea salt and olive oil, then place under a medium grill.
- Turn the prawns several times so that they are thoroughly cooked on both sides.
- When the prawns are golden, place on a serving dish with the garlic mayonnaise to one side.

❝ *The Christmas Eve meal is never rushed, and consists of many courses. Typically, starters may be shellfish or prawns in mayonnaise with cold cuts of meat.* ❞

From *Two Old Fools - Olé!*

FRIED CHORIZO WITH APPLE AND CIDER

TAPAS
MEAT
EASY

An easy and quick tapas recipe with a very big flavour. Sweet caramelised apple slices cooked in the chorizo juices go deliciously well with the spicy sausage. Can be served hot or cold and is sure to keep the guests guessing.

Ingredients (6 servings)

3 chorizo sausages
1 apple (sweet)
300ml (half a pint) Asturian cider
1 bay leaf
Olive oil

Method

- Slice the chorizo sausages into half-inch segments.
- Pour a little olive oil into a frying pan and heat.
- Add the chorizo segments and cook for 1 minute each side over a low heat.
- Meanwhile, slice the apple into 12 segments.
- Add the apple, bay leaf and cider to the chorizo.
- Turn up the heat and cook until the cider begins to thicken.
- Serve hot with cocktail sticks.

" *Mama Ufarte and Lola drifted in and out of their house, collecting tapas and bread, and laying them out on the table they'd prepared. Lola seemed a little sulky, and I guessed it was because Geronimo was too wrapped up in the approaching game to pay her much attention.* "

From *Two Old Fools - Olé!*

FRIED CHORIZO IN GARLIC

TAPAS
MEAT
EASY

Chorizo braises well, is good for kebabs and fries beautifully. This recipe has a simple combination of chorizo and garlic, lightly fried in olive oil. Delicious Spanish tapas and ready in under 5 minutes.

Ingredients

2 chorizo sausages (150g or 6 oz)

2 garlic cloves

Olive oil

Crusty bread

Method

- Take 2 chorizo sausages and slice thinly into 8 to 10 segments each.
- Peel the garlic cloves and cut into 8 to 10 slices each.
- Heat a drizzle of olive oil in a frying pan and fry the chorizo for 1 minute.
- Add the sliced garlic and fry with the chorizo pieces for a further 2 minutes or until the garlic begins to turn golden brown.
- Remove the ingredients from the pan.
- Lay them to rest on a sheet of kitchen towel.
- Serve in small tapas bowls along with salad or peppered tomatoes.
- Retain the infused olive oil and use for further cooking or enjoy with fresh crusty bread.

" *It's my birthday, and it's also the British Grand Prix, Moto GP and the World Cup final. All in one day. I'm going to watch all of them and Vicky's promised to serve me tapas, naked."*

"I most certainly did not!". "

From *Two Old Fools - Olé!*

SHERRIED CHORIZO

TAPAS
MEAT
FAIRLY EASY

This chorizo tapas recipe is incredibly easy and quick to make and is packed full of flavour. Use spicy chorizos for a fiery kick, accompanied with Fino de Jerez sherry.

Ingredients (makes 6 tapas)

3 chorizo sausages
1 Spanish onion, diced
3 garlic cloves, chopped
Half teaspoon hot paprika
250ml (half pint) fino de Jerez sherry
Parsley
Cracked black pepper
Olive oil

Method

- Lightly fry the onion in olive oil until it begins to brown.
- Meanwhile, slice the chorizo into half-inch pieces, and add to the softened onions in the pan.
- Fry for a further couple of minutes.
- Add the garlic, paprika and sherry to the onion and chorizo and cook until the sherry is reduced.
- Add a cup of warm water then simmer for 10 minutes.
- When the mixture has thickened add the parsley, season with pepper and stir well.
- Serve on tapas plates with fresh crusty bread and peppered vine tomatoes with olive oil.

> *Papa Ufarte leaped onto the table, feet oblivious to the plates of tapas, fists clenched, roaring, "GOAL!" at the sky.*
>
> *Paco stood on his doorstep with a bundle of fireworks, releasing giant rockets that ripped into the heavens.*
>
> From *Two Old Fools - Olé!*

SPANISH CHORIZO AND CALAMARI SALAD

TAPAS
MEAT
FAIRLY EASY

If you enjoy seafood and have a passion for Spanish chorizo, then this simple healthy salad is a real Mediterranean treat.

Ingredients

3 large whole squid

Good bunch of baby spinach leaves

150g (6 oz) sliced chorizo sausage

Extra virgin olive oil

Method

- Wash and clean the spinach leaves and place in a large bowl or cazuela.
- Clean the squid, remove the heads and cut the bodies into large squares.
- Score the meat to create a nice criss-cross effect for presentation.
- Thinly slice two chorizos.
- Fry the squid and chorizo in olive oil for 5 to 6 minutes.
- Place over the spinach leaves.
- Drizzle with extra virgin olive oil and salt and pepper to taste.

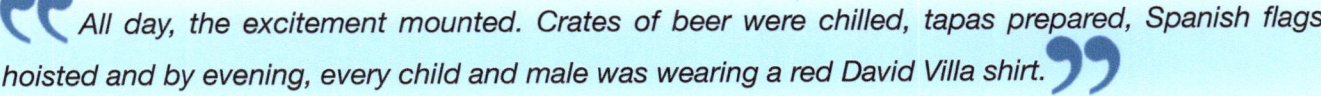

All day, the excitement mounted. Crates of beer were chilled, tapas prepared, Spanish flags hoisted and by evening, every child and male was wearing a red David Villa shirt.

From *Two Old Fools - Olé!*

DEVILLED KIDNEY AND WILD MUSHROOM TOSTADA

TAPAS
MEAT
SOME SKILL

The tostada is a typical Spanish breakfast enjoyed in bars all over Spain, and you will see workers eating tostada de tomate most mornings. The humble tostada lends itself well to a whole variety of toppings. In this recipe there are pigs' kidneys (although lambs' kidneys work equally well) and mixed wild mushrooms. Together with a little smoked paprika, this hearty tostada will keep you going until lunchtime!

Ingredients (serves 2)

Half a stick of French bread

200g (8 oz) mixed mushrooms, quartered

1 pig's kidney (or 4 lambs' kidneys)

50g (2 oz) butter

1 tablespoon plain flour

¼ teaspoon hot smoked paprika

Salt

Cracked black pepper

Parsley

Method

- Slice the French stick horizontally and toast on both sides. Leave to cool.
- Melt half the butter in a frying pan and fry the mushrooms. When done, set aside and keep warm.
- Meanwhile, slice the kidney lengthways, but not all the way through. Open like a book then cut into strips.
- Add the paprika to the flour and season with salt and pepper, dust the sliced kidney ensuring a good covering.
- Melt the remaining butter in the frying pan and fry the kidney for 2 minutes turning regularly.
- Reintroduce the mushrooms for 30 seconds and mix with the kidney.
- Butter the toast, then spoon over the ingredients.
- Garnish with torn parsley before serving.

> Buy one loaf of bread, get another two free. Buy a case of beer, get a free parasol. If we refused the free gifts, the assistants would be affronted, so we had a freezer full of surplus bread and an ever-growing pile of yellow San Miguel parasols in our garage.
>
> From *Two Old Fools - Olé!*

HARISSA
Spicy Chili Sauce

TAPAS — EASY

It's recommended that you wear washing-up gloves when chopping the chilies or you could be subjected to some very unpleasant experiences!

A jar of this may be kept in the fridge, but do cover it with more olive oil to preserve it.

Ingredients (makes about 225g or 8 oz)

175g (6 oz) fresh red chilies

2 tsp tomato purée

4 tbsp canned pimento, chopped.

4 garlic cloves, peeled

2 tsp each of ground coriander and ground caraway seeds

1 tsp ground cumin

Salt

2 tsp red wine vinegar

Olive oil

Method

- Remove the seeds from the chilies if you don't want it too hot!
- Chop the chilies and place in a blender (or pestle and mortar).
- Add all the rest of the ingredients and a couple of glugs of olive oil.
- Blend until you have a smooth paste.
- Check the seasoning.

HOT POTATOES WITH A WHITE BEAN AND SHERRY GARLIC DIP

TAPAS
VEGETARIAN
EASY

A lovely smooth, blended dip for hot potato wedges that also goes exceptionally well with raw vegetables such as carrots, celery and summer salads. Great for the tapas table!

Ingredients (serves 2)

2 - 3 large potatoes
200g (7 oz) jar of white beans
1 garlic clove
200ml (6 to 7 fl oz) water
Pinch of cracked black pepper
250ml (half pint) extra virgin olive oil
Splash of sherry vinegar
Salt to taste

Method

- Cut the potatoes into wedges and place into a fryer and cook, or parboil and fry in olive oil.
- Meanwhile, place all of the other ingredients into a blender and blend for a good 60 seconds until a smooth paste is achieved.
- Taste test, adding more garlic or sherry vinegar to achieve your preferred flavour strength. Add a little more olive oil if required.
- Pour into a bowl or *cazuela* and serve with the hot potato wedges or salad.
- Tip: Add half a teaspoon of hot smoked paprika for an extra smoky flavour.

Villagers nibbled on the tapas and stood chatting in clusters. Elderly couples danced together, while children ran in and out of the huge open entry gates.

From *Two Old Fools - Olé!*

JAKE'S DAD'S THANKSGIVING SWEET POTATO WONDERFUL

SIDE DISH
VEGETARIAN
SOME SKILL

It may seem a little strange to some Europeans to serve sweet potatoes topped with marshmallows as a side dish with a traditional roast turkey dinner. However, it is a delicious dish and can easily be served as a dessert if you prefer.

Ingredients

7 lbs (3 kilos) of sweet potatoes

⅓ cup of brown sugar (could add more, depending on how sweet you like it)

1 stick of butter (softened but not melted) (4 oz or 113g)

1 10.5 oz (300g) package of miniature marshmallows

½ tablespoon of cinnamon

(Salt to taste…approx 3 teaspoons)

1 teaspoon of nutmeg (optional)

¼ cup of sliced almonds to add texture and some interest.

(Optional…but a very delicious addition, is to add a streusel type topping. You can buy a packaged mix at most US grocery stores.)

Method

- After rinsing off potatoes, slice up sweet potatoes into thirds (each section about ½ the size of a green pepper). With skin still on, boil potatoes for approximately 15 minutes. Stick fork in potato for softness.
- Remove from heat when fork enters with no resistance, but potato should not fall apart.
- With potatoes still in the pan, pour out hot water and add cold water with just a few cubes of ice to help cool potatoes enough to be able to peel them. Let cool in pan for two or three minutes.
- Begin to pull off peel and place potatoes in large mixing bowl. (Peel should come off easily.)
- Mash using a potato masher.
- Add brown sugar, butter, cinnamon, salt, nutmeg, and sliced almonds. Stir until smooth.
- Spread out half of the mixture into the baking pan and smooth the top using a spatula.
- Sprinkle half of the marshmallows over the mixture and finish covering with the remaining potato mix.
- If you are going to use a crumbly topping (streusel), apply it as the top layer at this time.
- Sprinkle extra almonds, if you like, but leave space to put on the final layer of marshmallows. The top of the mixture should never be above the top of the baking dish.
- Bake at 350°F (180°C) for approximately 15 minutes.
- Take out mixture and add final layer of marshmallows. Bake mixture for another 5 - 10 minutes… just enough time to get marshmallows on top time to brown.
- Take out and let cool for 10 minutes…time to serve the WONDERFUL!

SPANISH ROASTED TOMATOES

**TAPAS
VEGETARIAN
EASY**

Serve as part of an outdoor buffet or side dish with barbecued chicken. This is also a perfect accompaniment to any tortilla dish.

Ingredients

12 large ripe vine tomatoes
3 tablespoons olive oil
2 tablespoons balsamic vinegar
A sprinkle of caster sugar

Method

- Halve the tomatoes and place in a single layer in a roasting tin.
- Drizzle with the oil and vinegar and mix well.
- Roast in a medium oven for around 45 minutes to an hour (adding the sugar after 20 minutes or so).
- When they are ready, they will be soft and lightly caramelised.
- Serve warm.

Paco's balled fist would pound on our front door, making us jump.

"English!" he'd bellow. "We have tomatoes for you!" (Or cherries, or shiny red and green peppers - depending on the season.) He'd hand us a huge bag crammed with produce while his wife, Carmen-Bethina, stood behind him, a broad smile dimpling her round cheeks.

From *Two Old Fools - Olé!*

SAMBOUSEK
Spinach Kisses

TAPAS
VEGETARIAN
SOME SKILL

As Nadia says, "This recipe will make loads of pastries, but none of them will ever make it to the freezer!"

Ingredients (makes 30 - 40 pastries)

10g (¼ oz) dried yeast

A pinch of caster sugar

300ml (½ pint) warm water

500g (1¼ lb) strong white bread flour

1 tbsp fine salt

6 tbsp olive oil

Melted butter, for brushing

For the filling:

500g (1¼ lb) fresh spinach, washed and thoroughly dried

2½ tsp fine salt

1 medium onion, peeled and finely chopped

2 tbsp olive oil

2 tbsp sumac (from Middle Eastern shops)

Large handful of pine nuts

Knob of butter

5 tbsp lemon juice

1 tsp freshly ground black pepper

Method

- Place the yeast and sugar in half the warm water and leave until it bubbles.
- Put the flour and salt in a large mixing bowl, making a well in the middle. Add the oil and yeast. Knead the dough for 15 - 20 minutes until soft.
- Add the rest of the water bit by bit; you may not need all of it.
- Place the bowl in a warm spot, with a cloth over it, for 1½ - 2 hours, until double in size.
- For the filling, put the spinach with 1 tsp of salt into a bowl. Rub them together until the spinach reduces down, then chop. (Don't cook it.)
- Fry the onion in the oil until transparent, then stir in the sumac.
- Mix the (uncooked) spinach with the onion.
- Fry the pine nuts separately in the butter until light golden brown. Stir these into the spinach with lemon juice and pepper.
- Preheat the oven to 180°C/gas mark 4/350°F and grease a couple of baking trays.
- Knead the dough a little and divide it into about 30 pieces. Roll them out into 7½ cm (3 inch) rounds.
- Place about 1 tsp of the spinach filling into the middle of each circle. With your finger, wet the edge of the circle and fold over the pastry, pinching it closed.
- Place the pastries on a baking tray and brush with butter. Bake for 20 - 30 minutes, until light golden. ("God, these are good!" says Nadia.)

ARABIC SALAD

**TAPAS
VEGETARIAN
EASY**

Nadia says, "I serve this lovely, fresh salad with meat, fish, chicken, baked potatoes and falafel. But, sometimes, without telling anyone, I just make a huge bowl of it and eat the lot entirely on its own!"

Ingredients (serves 4)

1 red onion, peeled and very thinly sliced.

Juice of 1 lemon

3 tomatoes, cubed

2 small Middle Eastern cucumbers, cubed

1 small Cos lettuce, chopped

1 small green pepper, seeded and thinly sliced

1 tbsp chopped fresh parsley

1 pita bread, cut into squares and fried in olive oil

For the dressing:

3 tbsp olive oil

3 tbsp lemon juice

1 garlic clove, peeled and crushed

1 tsp sumac (from Middle Eastern shops, and many big stores)

1 tbsp chopped fresh mint

Salt

Method

- Macerate the red onion in the lemon juice for 10 minutes.
- For the dressing, put the oil, lemon juice and garlic in a small bowl, and stir well.
- Now add the remaining ingredients.
- Place all the vegetables into a bowl.
- Just before serving, add the fried pita bread, and pour the dressing over it.

Sue Franey, chef and photographer of the Old Fools' recipes

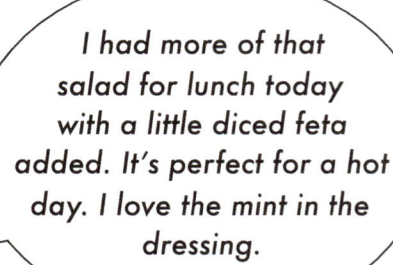

I had more of that salad for lunch today with a little diced feta added. It's perfect for a hot day. I love the mint in the dressing.

SECTION 2

FISH, MEAT AND VEGETARIAN DISHES

BARBECUED SARDINES

FISH

EASY

Just three ingredients and a barbecue is all you need for this wonderful summer dish.

Ingredients (serves 4)

8 medium to large sardines

Handful fresh parsley

Salt to season

Method

- Clean the sardines and remove the heads, then wash under running water.
- Cook on a barbecue or under the grill for a few minutes each side until cooked through.
- Season with salt and garnish with a squeeze of lemon juice and fresh chopped parsley.

"We don't need two, we can share one," said Nicholas.

"But will that be enough?" Caroline worried.

"Well, we can choose a big one." Then, to the assistant, "That one, please. No, the one behind it. Oh, that's bigger than I thought - maybe the one on the left, no, perhaps the next one..."

And so it continued until they were both finally satisfied and the weighed, wrapped fish was handed over like a newborn baby. The assistant and I were united in relief. I sped the trolley away before they could change their minds again."

From *Chickens, Mules and Two Old Fools*

TUNA WITH A SPICY SAUCE
Atún con Salsa

FISH — EASY

There are so many ways to cook tuna, but this recipe with hot paprika and garlic is a big hit with us.

Ingredients

2 large fresh tuna steaks or 4 small ones

6 garlic cloves

3 tablespoons olive oil

1 teaspoon hot paprika

Salt and pepper

Method

- Grill the unpeeled garlic until they become soft.
- Allow to cool a little, then cut the end off each garlic clove and squeeze the garlic flesh into a bowl.
- Add the paprika, olive oil, salt and pepper to the bowl and mix well.
- Place the tuna steaks into a shallow dish, pour over the above sauce and leave to marinade for about half an hour.
- Cook on a barbecue or grill for about 5-6 minutes each side.
- Serve with a salad and boiled potatoes.

Oh my Lord! Absolutely loved this tuna in spicy sauce! It was a real winner.

Sue Franey, chef and photographer of the Old Fools' recipes

> *To this day, none of us has ever mentioned the incident of Thief Cat and the stolen fish again.*
>
> From *Chickens, Mules and Two Old Fools*

MACKEREL FILLETS IN GARLIC AND PAPRIKA

FISH — EASY

Spanish mackerel recipe using some traditional Spanish ingredients. This dish is great served with summer salad, boiled vegetables or simply with fresh crusty bread.

Ingredients

2 mackerel fillets
3 cloves of garlic (sliced)
Broadleaf parsley
1 teaspoon smoked paprika
Splash of red wine vinegar
Salt
Cracked black pepper
Extra virgin olive oil

Method

- Heat up some olive oil in frying pan, add the mackerel fillets and fry for 2 to 3 minutes, skin side down.
- Turn the fish over, season and cook for an additional 60 seconds.
- When the fish is cooked, remove from the pan and plate up ready to serve.
- Add a splash more olive oil to the frying pan, then throw in the garlic, parsley, vinegar, pepper and paprika. Mix and fry for 1 minute.
- Pour the mixture over the mackerel fillets and serve.

> "The Ufartes? Related to the Fish Man? Lord! I know that family well! I'll bet they're noisy! You don't let those little vandals play football in your garden, do you?"
> "Well, yes. I mean, no..."

From *Two Old Fools - Olé!*

BAKED MACKEREL

FISH
EASY

A very popular Spanish recipe for baked mackerel, which is cooked in the oven with ripe tomatoes and potatoes. Full of herbs and spices, this dish makes a lovely healthy lunch or supper.

Ingredients

4 large mackerel fish cleaned and cut into thirds

3 potatoes, peeled and cut into bite-sized chunks

4 large ripe tomatoes quartered

4 cloves garlic peeled and cut in half

3 large glasses white wine

Olive oil

Handful of fresh parsley, roughly chopped

Salt and Pepper

Method

- Place the mackerel, tomatoes, potatoes and garlic in a large oven-proof dish and drizzle with a little olive oil.
- Pour the wine over and sprinkle with the parsley.
- Season with salt and pepper.
- Cook in a moderate oven for 40 to 50 minutes until the mackerel is cooked through but still moist.

“When the fish van hooted its horn at the top of the mountain road, as many as thirty cats would magically appear outside Marcia's shop, along with the village ladies, awaiting the arrival of the fish van.”

From *Two Old Fools - Olé!*

LEMON SWORDFISH WITH ROASTED TOMATOES

FISH
EASY

Swordfish steaks go well with salads and potatoes, or roasted tomatoes. Buy the biggest, ripest tomatoes you can get, as they'll roast slightly quicker. Served with lashings of extra virgin olive oil and fresh bread, you can't get much more Mediterranean than this!

Ingredients (serves 2)

2 swordfish steaks
2 large tomatoes
A squeeze of lemon juice
Parsley
Ground black pepper
Extra virgin olive oil

Method

- Quarter each tomato, place on a baking tray and oven roast on a high heat 220°C (420°F) for 30 minutes.
- Ten minutes before the tomatoes are ready, heat some olive oil in a pan, add the swordfish steaks and squeeze over with lemon juice.
- Lightly fry for 4 minutes each side.
- Arrange the swordfish on a plate with the roast tomato segments.
- Season with black pepper and add a generous splash of good olive oil.
- Garnish with parsley and serve with fresh crusty bread.

" She seemed to survive well enough, scrounging fish scraps from the fish van, hunting sparrows and lizards, and raiding whenever the opportunity arose. "

From *Two Old Fools - Olé!*

AMOROSO MUSSELS WITH ALMONDS

SEAFOOD
SOME SKILL

This recipe for mussels uses Spanish Amoroso sherry, a change from white wine, and produces a real depth of flavour to the shellfish. Almonds are also scattered over the mussels whilst steaming. The mussels are then served in bowls and garnished with parsley.

Ingredients (serves 4)

1.5kg (3lb 4 oz) fresh mussels

3 garlic cloves, thinly sliced

50g (2 oz) butter

75ml (5 tbs) Amoroso sherry

Juice of half a lemon

30g (1 - 2 oz) toasted almonds, crushed

Parsley

Method

- Melt the butter in a large deep pan. Cook the garlic for 2 minutes.
- Tip your cleaned mussels into the pan, add the sherry and almonds and squeeze over the lemon juice.
- Using a wooden spoon, stir the mussels well to mix in the ingredients.
- Steam for 4 to 5 minutes until mussels have opened.
- Spoon the mussels into bowls adding a tablespoon or two of the mussel liquid from the pan.
- Garnish with chopped parsley and serve.

❝Most families owned one of these machines, and the noise of almonds being de-husked filled the village. Nothing was wasted. The families ate or sold the almonds, and the husks were fed to the goats.❞
From *Two Old Fools - Olé!*

GARLIC PRAWNS WITH SMOKED PAPRIKA
Gambas al Ajillo con Pimentón

SEAFOOD — FAIRLY EASY

This recipe comes from 'Mouth-Watering Spanish Recipes', a book I co-wrote with Gayle MacDonald. It's one of our favourite tapas dishes that goes well with a cold beer, or as a supper snack. It combines some beautiful, authentic Spanish flavours, like prawns from the Mediterranean, Fino sherry from Jerez, and smoked paprika. A combination that can be enjoyed at any time and is particularly delicious eaten outdoors.

Ingredients (serves 4)

1 kg (2.2lbs) prawns
4 garlic cloves, peeled and chopped
Olive oil
Black pepper
1 teaspoon hot smoked paprika
Splash of Fino sherry

Method

- Thoroughly wash the prawns. Peel, leaving the tails on.
- Heat a generous slug of olive oil in a large terracotta cazuela or pan.
- Add garlic, paprika and sherry, and fry for 2 minutes to infuse the olive oil.
- Add prawns, season with black pepper and fry, turning regularly for 4 minutes, or until cooked through.
- Serve on a bed of salad accompanied by fresh, crusty bread.

We invited some friends round for tapas.

Sue Franey, chef and photographer of the Old Fools' recipes

CHICKEN AND PRAWN PAELLA
Paella Mixta

MIXED
SOME SKILL

There are numerous paella recipes which makes choosing just one difficult. This is a particularly delicious one, with chicken breasts and prawns.

Ingredients (serves 8 - 10)

2 skinless boneless chicken breasts

500g (18 oz) uncooked prawns

3 tablespoons olive oil

1 medium onion

2 cloves garlic

1 medium red pepper

1 medium green pepper

2 large tomatoes

150g (5 oz) fresh frozen garden peas

500g (18 oz) paella rice

1 ltr (2 pints) chicken stock

¼ teaspoon saffron

Salt and pepper

Method

- Peel and clean the prawns and cut the chicken into bite-sized pieces.
- Peel and chop the onion and garlic, chop the peppers and tomatoes.
- Heat the olive oil in a medium paella pan, add the garlic and onion and cook gently until soft then add the chicken and cook until browned on all sides.
- Add the peppers and cook for 5 minutes.
- Meanwhile, heat the chicken stock.
- Add the tomatoes and cook for 5 minutes.
- Add the rice using a soup ladle, counting as you go (you need to add 3 parts water to one part rice) and cook for 5 minutes.
- Add the chicken stock again ladle by ladle, season and bring to the boil. (Do not stir).
- Reduce the heat, cover and simmer for 15 minutes or so.
- Then add the prawns, peas and the saffron and continue cooking for a further 10 - 15 minutes until the liquid has been absorbed.
- Turn off the heat, cover and leave to rest for 5 minutes before serving.
- Garnish with fresh chopped parsley.

MEDITERRANEAN ROAST CHICKEN

MEAT
EASY

A lovely Mediterranean-style roast chicken, with lots of herbs and seasonal vegetables. The best thing about this dish is that it just goes into the oven and cooks itself!

Ingredients

1 whole medium fresh chicken

2 green or red peppers

2 medium onions

1 medium courgette

3 tomatoes

150g (5 - 6 oz) mushrooms

Oregano

Thyme

Olive oil

Salt and pepper

Method

- Wash the chicken inside and out, removing any giblets, and pat dry. Place in a large oiled roasting tin.
- Rub the outside of the chicken with olive oil, season with a little salt and pepper and sprinkle generously with oregano and thyme.
- Cook in a high oven for about 20 minutes, basting with the juices.
- Prepare the vegetables by washing and/or peeling and chopping into chunks.
- Add the vegetables to the pan and lower the heat on the oven to medium, then cook for an hour to an hour and a half, depending on the size of the chicken.
- Check the chicken is done by inserting a thin knife between the leg and breast. If the juices run clear, then the chicken is cooked. If not, then leave for another 20 minutes.
- Serve immediately with boiled potatoes or lots of fresh bread to mop up the juices.

Oh my lord, this Mediterranean roast chicken is just the best!

Sue Franey, chef and photographer of the Old Fools' recipes

❝ We couldn't find turkey or Brussels sprouts in our supermarket, standard fare on a British Christmas table, so we had roast chicken and as many trimmings as we could find. ❞

From *Two Old Fools - Olé!*

GARLIC AND PEPPER CHICKEN

MEAT
EASY

A hot and spicy chicken recipe using chicken pieces, great with thighs, drumsticks, or breast and packs a real fiery punch. Ideal for the oven or barbecue. Can be eaten hot or cold.

Ingredients

8 chicken pieces (skinned)
10 garlic cloves (crushed)
1 large sprig fresh thyme
1 pinch rosemary
1 tablespoon hot smoked paprika
1 tablespoon cracked black peppercorns
Splash of Fino sherry
Olive oil

Method

- Clean and skin the chicken pieces and place on a baking tray.
- In a pestle and mortar add a generous drizzle of olive oil and the garlic, herbs, pepper, paprika and sherry.
- Crush and mix well, adding more olive oil if required to create a paste.
- Spoon the mixture over the chicken pieces.
- Cook in the oven on a medium heat for 35 - 40 minutes.
- Serve with chips, fritters or salad.

> *I reached into the back of the barbecue, and winkled out the kittens, one by one. Then I carried each carefully back to the straw-filled box in the wood-shed. The two girls cried and fought all the way, but the little chap sat in my hands, calmly surveying his surroundings.*
>
> From *Two Old Fools - Ole!*

SLOW-COOKED BRANDY CHICKEN

MEAT

EASY

Beautiful served with fresh crispy salad, boiled potatoes, bread and olive oil.

Ingredients (serves 4)

4 chicken legs, separated into thighs and drumsticks

1 and a half bulbs of garlic

Reasonable size glass brandy

1 bay leaf

Olive oil

Salt

Pepper

Paprika (mild or hot)

Method

- Sprinkle the chicken with a generous amount of salt, pepper and paprika, then rub the seasoning into the chicken and leave to rest for about 20 minutes. Peel and roughly chop the garlic.
- Heat a little olive oil in a large casserole dish and slowly brown the chicken pieces on both sides. Add the garlic about halfway through this step.
- When the chicken is browned, add the brandy and bay leaf.
- Cover and cook gently until the chicken is tender, about 30 - 40 minutes depending on the size of the pieces.
- Serve with rice, boiled potatoes or a salad.

❝Joe was so indignant, so outraged, that it took all my wifely skills plus a generous medicinal brandy to calm him. As he simmered down, still spluttering and cursing, I checked something.❞

From *Two Old Fools - Olé!*

HONEY BARBECUED CHICKEN

MEAT
EASY

Served with a glass of white Rioja, this summer dish is light, versatile and goes down well with salads or cold potatoes.

Ingredients

4 skinless chicken breasts
Juice of 1 lemon
2 tablespoons of honey
2 garlic cloves (crushed)
Knob of butter

Method

- Melt the butter in a cazuela or pan and cook the garlic for 1 minute.
- Mix in the lemon juice and honey, keeping some aside for basting the chicken breasts later.
- Marinate the chicken in the mixture for an hour.
- Prepare the barbecue creating a good brasa or even level of hot coals.
- Place the chicken on the barbecue and cook for 15 minutes turning frequently.
- Baste the chicken generously 2 minutes before serving.

"First she gave her baby a good wash, then she scruffed it, and leaped back onto the barbecue, the fat little kitten dangling limply from her mouth. The kitten seemed unhurt in spite of the perilous drop and the undignified landing on the unforgiving paving stones below."

I shook my head. No, the barbecue was not a good choice, even Joe agreed.

From *Two Old Fools - Olé!*

THE GIN TWINS' CHUCK-IT-ALL-IN CURRY

| MEAT |
| EASY |

- **Juliet:** Well, I think we use about two onions chopped and softened in the pan with about 3 cloves of garlic crushed and added to the onion.

Then you need 4 chicken breasts, chopped into cubes, add to onion and cook all over. Then we add a tablespoon of curry paste and a few teaspoons of curry powder. Also need a couple of red peppers!

A nice gin and tonic for the chefs is a good idea at this stage.

We then add some water, a tin of chopped tomatoes and a large glug of wine!

You need to peel 4 medium potatoes and dice them and add to pan, along with some chopped cauliflower, carrot and whatever other veg is in Vicky's fridge.

Oh, add a tin of sweet corn too. The whole lot is left to simmer for a few hours. Add water or more curry powder if necessary!

Ok, Sue, have I forgotten anything? Oh yes, you need to drink gin.

- **Sue:** And top tip for cooking rice, wash rice thoroughly in a sieve under running water until water is clear.

Place washed rice in bowl and cover well with water. Leave for up to an hour. Drain then cook in boiling water for about 10 minutes. Perfect fluffy rice every time!

Health warning on curry cooking, avoid cooking poppadoms after drinking gin...

- **Juliet:** Forgot to say we add whole chilies and if we can't get them, then chili powder.
- **Sue:** Absolutely!
- **Juliet:** Had to add that, it's been bugging me! We couldn't have a Fail in the curry department.

> *The Gin Twins were in full singing voice while I concentrated on driving. I was a little concerned. Instead of calming, the wind seemed to be growing in strength. Sharp blasts rocked the jeep and made the Gin Twins squeal. Branches and debris littered the dark road.*
>
> From *Chickens, Mules and Two Old Fools*

SHISH TAOUK
Thyme For Kebabs

MEAT

FAIRLY EASY

Nadia calls this delicious dish, 'It's Thyme for Kebabs'. It is best barbecued but can also be grilled and should take the same amount of time. Remember to first soak wooden skewers in water to prevent them from catching fire. Traditionally, this dish is made with chicken breasts, but boned thigh meat is also really tasty. The longer you leave the meat to marinate, the more tender and delicious it will be.

Ingredients (serves 8)

4 boneless, skinned chicken breasts, diced into 2½ cm (1 inch) cubes

6 boned chicken thighs, cubed as above

For the marinade

6 - 8 garlic cloves, peeled and pounded until creamy

Juice of 4 lemons

1 handful fresh thyme

1 tsp cayenne pepper

A few glugs of olive oil

Lots of crunchy salt

Method

- Have your barbecue coals ready, and your wooden skewers soaking in water.
- Thoroughly mix the marinade ingredients in a small bowl.
- Place the breast and thigh meat in 2 separate bowls. Share out the marinade ingredients between them and mix well.
- Allow to marinate for at least 15 minutes, but the longer the better.
- Thread the breasts and thighs on separate skewers.
- Place the skewers on hot, white coals.
- Regularly baste and turn, until cooked through and golden (takes about 8 minutes).
- Serve in a wrap of hot flatbread with a drizzle of tahini sauce.

MUSSAKHAN
Roast Chicken on a Magic Carpet

MEAT
SOME SKILL

Nadia describes this as, "Roasted Chicken on a Magical Carpet of Bread, Onions and Sumac". This delicious dish is perfect, especially if careful attention is paid to the slow cooking of the onions. Shrak bread (available from Middle Eastern shops or online) is preferable but may be replaced with tortilla wraps or even pita bread.

Top Tip: Prepare the onion mixture the day before and marinate the chicken pieces with it.

Ingredients (serves 4)

8 chicken pieces, dried with paper towel

2 tbsp vegetable oil

Shrak bread (or tortilla wraps, or pita bread)

For the onion mixture

6 - 8 good glugs of olive oil

8 large onions, sliced

125ml (4 fl oz) chicken stock

A pinch of caster sugar

8 - 10 tbsp sumac (berry-red, available from Middle Eastern shops)

Method

- Heat the olive oil in a large frying pan.
- Throw in the onions, with salt, and cook really slowly for 20 - 25 minutes, stirring frequently.
- When soft and glistening, add the stock, stir, and allow to bubble a little.
- Add the sugar and stir continuously.
- Add the sumac and stir continuously.
- Preheat the oven to 180°C/Gas mark 4.
- Brown the chicken pieces in the vegetable oil.
- Line the tin, or *cazuela*, or baking dish, with a couple of layers of shrak bread and half the onion mixture.
- Lay the chicken on this and cover with the rest of the onion mixture.
- If you have time, leave to marinate again.
- Place in the oven for 20 - 25 minutes or until the chicken is cooked through.
- Serve with steamed rice, garnished with pine nuts and almonds, yoghurt and a green salad.

LAMB COCHIFRITO

MEAT
SOME SKILL

Lamb Cochifrito originally came from Northern Spain but is a popular dish in Andalucía today, found on many restaurant menus. Adding a splash of cream works very well with the paprika.

Ingredients

1 kg (2lb 4oz) lamb steaks
1 onion (chopped)
1 green pepper (chopped)
2 garlic cloves (crushed)
1 teaspoon smoked paprika
Juice of half a lemon
Salt and pepper
Broadleaf parsley

Method

- First, take the lamb steaks and remove the bone from the centre, then slice the meat into strips.
- Heat a little olive oil in a large cazuela or frying pan and add the lamb. Cook until browned then add the onion and fry for a further 2 minutes.
- Add the garlic, green pepper, smoked paprika and lemon juice, reduce heat and cook for 15 - 20 minutes.
- Season with salt and pepper.
- Serve and garnish with roughly chopped parsley.

This was a bit of a challenge to photograph but I did my best. Tasted yummy though.

Sue Franey, chef and photographer of the Old Fools' recipes

" *Saucepans steamed on the hob and a cauldron bubbled on the tripod over the open fire.* "
From *Two Old Fools - Olé*

SHEIKH-AL-MAHSHI LAMB-STUFFED PEPPERS AND AUBERGINES

MEAT
SOME SKILL

Nadia says that this is known throughout the Arab world as 'the king of the stuffed ones'.

Ingredients (serves 2 - 4)

4 small aubergines

4 green peppers

Olive oil

1 large onion, peeled and finely minced

1 large garlic clove, peeled and finely chopped

2 tbsp pine nuts

900g (2lb) minced lamb (not too finely minced)

2 tsp ground allspice

A bunch of fresh parsley, chopped

Salt and black pepper

2 tbsp tomato purée

600ml (1 pint) water (or enough to cover the vegetables)

Method

- Preheat the oven to 190°C/gas mark 5/375°F.
- Remove the leaves and make a slit down one side of the aubergines from top to bottom. Note: If the aubergine is curved, make the slit on the concave side.
- Scoop out the flesh, leaving a 5mm (¼ inch) shell all the way around.
- Discard the flesh.

(Continued)

- Cut round the tops of the peppers, leaving 2.5cm (1 inch) uncut so that you can re-attach it.
- Scoop out and discard the seeds.
- In a large pan, fry the aubergine and pepper shells until they begin to brown, and remove from the pan.
- Add a little more oil to the pan and fry the onion and garlic until they're soft. Remove from the pan.
- Fry the pine nuts. Remove from the pan.
- Next fry the lamb, with the spice, until it just begins to brown.
- At the end, throw in a big handful of parsley and stir.
- Now add the onions and garlic back, together with the pine nuts, salt, and plenty of black pepper, and mix together.
- Fully stuff (without pressure) this mixture into the aubergines and peppers.
- Close the lids on the peppers. and arrange the aubergines and peppers together in a shallow ovenproof dish.
- Mix the tomato purée, seasoned with salt and pepper with just enough water to cover the vegetables.
- Pour this over the vegetables and bake until tender, about 30 minutes. (The sauce should reduce to halfway down.)
- Sprinkle with the remaining chopped parsley.

BARBECUED SPANISH LAMB

MEAT
FAIRLY EASY

A real treat in the summer time. This delicate, yet flavoursome, marinade is best left for at least three hours to infuse. Use lamb chops or a leg of lamb cut into steaks, or a full leg that has been boned and flattened.

Ingredients

1 leg of lamb, cut into thick chops

Generous handful of fresh mint

1 onion, peeled and grated

1 clove of garlic, peeled and crushed

Dry mustard

Freshly ground black pepper

200g butter

Method

- Rub each chop with the pepper and dry mustard then place a layer of mint leaves in a large shallow dish.
- Add the lamb and cover with grated onion and more mint leaves. Leave in the fridge for at least three hours.
- In a saucepan, combine the butter and garlic and cook gently for 5 minutes then add a little more fresh chopped mint and simmer for a few minutes more.
- Remove the lamb from the dish, removing all of the mint leaves, and place on the barbecue grill.
- Brush the lamb with the garlic butter sauce during cooking, about 6 to 8 minutes each side.
- Serve immediately with a sprinkle of salt for juicy, succulent lamb with a delicate hint of mint and garlic.

❝ *Mountainous piles of wooden pallets, old furniture, logs and bits of timber sprout up on the beach all day. Barbecues are set up and when night falls, the crowds arrive in droves.* ❞

From Two Old Fools - Olé

SPICED LAMB AND DATE TAGINE

MEAT
SOME SKILL

Although this fabulous recipe is best cooked in a traditional tagine or other clay dish, like the Spanish *cazuela*, it may also be prepared in a heavy-based pan.

Ingredients (serves 4)

1kg (2¼ lb) leg of lamb

A dollop of butter

2 tbsp olive oil

1 medium onion, peeled and thinly sliced

2 tsp each of ground cinnamon and ground ginger

500ml (18 fl oz) water

3 tbsp chopped dates

Salt and black pepper

2 tbsp runny honey

2 tbsp lemon juice

To serve

8 fresh dates, stoned

55g (2 oz) whole shelled almonds, toasted

1 tbsp sesame seeds, toasted

Method

Cut the lamb into even cubes of about 4 cm (1½ inches) or ask your friendly butcher to do it for you.

Melt the butter and oil together in a tagine, *cazuela* or heavy-based pan. Seal the meat on all sides.

Add the onions, cooking them really slowly, translucent.

Add the spices and stir until their aroma is released.

Add the water and chopped dates.

Season well, cover and allow to cook for 1 - 1½ hours until the meat is soft. (If you are using a *cazuela*, use aluminium foil to create a lid.)

To finish, stir in the honey and lemon juice.

Scatter on the fresh dates and sprinkle on the toasted almonds and sesame seeds.

Serve with crusty bread to mop up the juices.

SPANISH MEATBALLS
Albóndigas

MEAT — SOME SKILL

Spanish meatballs appear on every restaurant menu in Spain, and it's obvious why. They are heavenly! In fact, this recipe is so delicious it deserves a double-page spread.

Ingredients (serves 4)

400g (14 oz) minced chicken

100g (4 oz) minced bacon

2 medium onions (one grated, one sliced)

1 carrot (grated)

I large tomato (chopped)

2 cloves garlic (chopped finely)

3 dessertspoons brown or white bread crumbs

1 glass white wine

1 bay leaf

Tomato puree

Half a stock cube

3 dessertspoons soy sauce

Handful of frozen peas

1 teaspoon fresh parsley (chopped)

I teaspoon oregano

Method - meat balls

- Mix the minced chicken with the bacon.
- Add the grated onion, half the chopped garlic, soy sauce, oregano and breadcrumbs.
- Mix well and roll the mixture into small balls.
- Roll these in the flour until coated, then set aside.

Sue Franey, chef and photographer of the Old Fools' recipes

They tasted amazing too. I used some home-smoked bacon which really boosted the flavour.

It doesn't matter whether I'm on a bar crawl in Madrid, Barcelona, San Sebastián or Seville, this is the little plate I'm looking for. Basically, I'm so friendly with albondigas I keep hoping one day they'll say, "You can call me Al."
This is an edited extract from
Yummy Easy Quick: Around the World
by Matt Preston. Published by Plum.

Method - sauce

- Heat a little olive oil in a frying pan and add the sliced onion, chopped garlic, parsley and pinch of salt and pepper.
- Fry gently for about 10 minutes until soft, then add the chopped tomato.
- Then grate and add the carrot.
- Dissolve the stock cube in a little water.
- Add this, the white wine, peas, a squirt of tomato puree and the bay leaf to the sauce.
- Stir well and allow to carry on simmering very gently.
- In another frying pan, heat enough oil to cover the bottom.
- Fry the meatballs until brown all over, keeping the meatballs moving and the heat low.
- As each batch of meatballs is cooked, add to the pan containing the sauce.
- When all the meatballs are fried and added, allow to simmer gently for half an hour.
- Serve hot with salad and crusty bread.

" *Dimples appeared in her round cheeks. She was pointing to three framed photos on the wall.*

"This one is Diego, he is thirty-two. He grows tomatoes, the best in Andalucía! Diego's tomatoes are sent all over the world, even England! These tomatoes we are eating now were grown by my son, Diego."

"They're very good," I said. "

From *Chickens, Mules and Two Old Fools*

SFEEHA
Middle Eastern Lamb Mini-Pizzas

MEAT
SOME SKILL

Nadia says this is her Auntie Jamileh's recipe, with a few little added ingredients of her own. Joe and I were often served these little pizzas at staff meetings in Bahrain. It's a delicious lunch with a salad, and any leftovers (unlikely) may be stored in the freezer.

Ingredients (makes 20 - 30)

For the topping

350g (12 oz) minced lamb

2 tsp each ground cinnamon and ground allspice

3 tbsp pine nuts, lightly fried

2 handfuls chopped fresh parsley

2 tsp pomegranate syrup (from Middle Eastern shops, online or large supermarkets)

1 - 2 tsp salt

1 tsp freshly ground black pepper

1 medium onion, peeled and grated

2 tomatoes, very finely chopped

4 tbsp tahini

2 tbsp lemon juice

For the dough

1 tsp dried yeast, dissolved with a pinch of caster sugar.

450g (1lb) strong white bread flour.

1½ tsp fine salt.

125ml (4 fl oz) olive oil

175ml (6 fl oz) plain yoghurt

125ml (4 fl oz) warm water

Method

- Place all topping materials in a bowl and mix until almost a paste. (Use your hands.) Put in the fridge.
- Leave the yeast for 5 minutes or until it starts to bubble.
- Place the flour and salt in a large bowl, making a well in the middle. Add the dissolved yeast, oil and yoghurt and mix well.
- Continue kneading, (a dough hook saves a lot of work) and adding a little warm water, until the dough is smooth and elastic.
- Roll the dough into a ball, place in a bowl, cover it and leave it in a warm place for 2 hours or until the dough has doubled in size.
- Punch it down and leave for another 20 - 30 minutes.
- Preheat the oven to 230°C /gas mark 8/450°F.
- On a floured surface, roll out the dough and divide it into about 30 pieces. Roll each out into a rough circle.
- Flatten a spoonful of the lamb mix onto each circle, right to the edge.
- Place the sfeeha onto a baking tray and then into the oven for 20 - 30 minutes. The dough should still be pale.

SHAWARMA
Marinated Lamb for Pita Tortilla or Wraps

MEAT — SOME SKILL

I had no idea what 'mastic' was, except as builders' putty stuff, but Nadia Sawalha's mum, Bobbie, enlightened me. Mastic is Arabic gum (not gum Arabic), and it's the resin from the mastic tree. Bobbie says the flavour is quite delicate, and mastic looks like cloudy sugar crystals about the size of round rice. It can be bought in small packets, online or from Turkish shops. She suggests that if you can't get it, just leave it out, as it can't be replaced by any other flavour.

Nadia claims that this delicious dish is divine when cooked on the barbecue, and will take only a minute or so to cook each side. If a barbecue is unavailable, then a really hot grill will do.

Top Tips: Grind the mastic finely between 2 spoons with a little sugar. Instead of pita bread, warmed tortilla can be used to wrap the ingredients in a tight hold-in-your-hand roll to eat.

Ingredients (serves 4 - 6)

450g (1lb) leg of lamb meat, cut into thin strips

2 tbsp cider vinegar

Juice of 1 juicy lemon

1 tsp finely grated lemon zest

1 tsp each of ground cinnamon and ground allspice

1 tsp each of salt and black pepper

½ tsp ground cardamom

3 pieces mastic (optional, see above)

1 small onion, peeled and grated

1 small tomato, chopped

3 glugs of olive oil

5 tbsp finely chopped fresh parsley

Method

- Place the shawarma ingredients in a bowl and leave in the fridge for 24 hours. Every now and then, give it a good stir.
- Remove from the fridge 1 hour before you need it. Allow to drain in a sieve or on a rack.
- Cook over a barbecue (or under a hot grill), giving each side a minute or so.
- Nestle the lamb into warmed pita bread, or onto a warmed tortilla.
- Add the salad and drizzle tahini sauce all over.

BEEF IN FRUIT SAUCE (ECUADORIAN RECIPE)
Carne Con Salsa de Frutas

MEAT — SOME SKILL

One glance at the ingredients that go into this dish will be enough to make you reach for your pan. Delicious!

Ingredients (serves 6)

3lbs (1.3 kilo) beef, cubed

1 large onion (chopped finely)

6 tablespoons vegetable oil

16 tablespoons beef stock

16 tablespoons dry white wine

16 tablespoons cream

2 peaches (peeled and chopped)

2 apples (peeled and chopped)

2 pears (peeled and chopped)

2 large tomatoes (peeled and chopped)

Salt, freshly ground pepper

Sugar to taste

Method

- Heat 4 tablespoons of oil in a frying pan and sauté onion.
- Transfer onion (use slotted spoon) to a casserole dish, and seal beef cubes quickly in remaining hot oil.
- Add to the casserole with the stock and wine.
- Season with salt and pepper.
- Cover, bring to the boil.
- Simmer on a low heat for approximately 2 hours, until meat is tender.
- Transfer beef (use slotted spoon) to a serving dish and keep it warm.
- Put stock aside.
- In a saucepan, heat remaining 2 tablespoons of oil.
- Add fruit, tomatoes and sugar. Cook for a few minutes, stirring continuously.
- Add enough of stock to just cover and simmer, stirring frequently.
- Allow to cool a little then blend, liquidise or sieve to a puree.
- Return the fruit puree to the saucepan.
- Add the cream and heat through. Do not allow to boil.
- Pour hot sauce over meat and serve with rice.

MARINATED SPANISH BEEF KEBABS

MEAT — EASY

Hot and spicy, ideal for the barbecue. Any vegetables, such as mushrooms, tomatoes, new potatoes, etc., can also be used.

Ingredients (serves 4)

2kg (4.5lb) beef (cubed)

4 garlic cloves

2 teaspoons hot smoked paprika

250ml (15 fl oz) olive oil

250ml (15 fl oz) wine vinegar

1 red bell pepper

1 large onion

Cracked black pepper

Thyme or mixed herbs

Method

- Place the cubed beef into a large dish and set aside.
- Using a food processor, blend together the garlic, herbs, pepper, vinegar, oil and paprika.
- Pour the spicy marinade over the beef and turn well so that all the meat is covered.
- Place in the fridge for a minimum of 2 hours.
- To make the kebabs, roughly chop the pepper and onion then thread over kebab sticks alternating with the beef.
- Retain any excess marinade as this will be used for basting the kebabs while on the grill.
- Barbecue the kebabs over hot coals for 10 to 12 minutes turning and basting frequently.
- Serve with fresh crispy salad, boiled potatoes, bread and olive oil.

> *"Joe, listen! Did you hear that?"*
>
> *"Yes, I did..."*
>
> So Joe and I played Follow the Squeak which led us to the barbecue. The barbecue was waist high, and below the grill was a metal box that Paco had welded for us. It was a lovely simple design: a box that holds burning charcoal, with grooves to rest one's kebab sticks.
>
> From *Two Old Fools - Olé!*

CHICKPEA AND CHORIZO SOUP
Garbanzos y Chorizo

MEAT — FAIRLY EASY

This dish was inspired by the Moors who introduced the chickpea or garbanzo. It is best using the *picante* (hot) chorizo to give it a fiery little Moroccan kick.

Ingredients (serves 6)

175g (6 oz) dried chickpeas

350g (12 oz) chorizo, diced into cubes about the same size as the chickpeas

1 onion, finely chopped

1 clove garlic, chopped or crushed

2 tbs olive oil

750ml (1.3 pints) chicken stock

1 bay leaf

Pinch of dried thyme

3 or 4 cloves

1 stick of cinnamon

1 tbs flat-leaf parsley

Method

- Cover the chickpeas with water in a bowl and leave to soak overnight.
- Drain and place in a large saucepan with the bay leaf, cloves and cinnamon stick.
- Add the stock and enough water to cover the peas completely.
- Bring to the boil then reduce the heat and simmer until the chickpeas are tender, approximately 1 hour. Do not allow to go soft or boil dry. Add more water if necessary.
- Drain and remove the herbs and spices.
- Meanwhile, medium heat the oil in a frying pan, add the chopped onion and cook gently until soft.
- Add the garlic and thyme and cook for about a minute.
- Turn up the heat a little and add the chorizo.
- Cook for about three minutes then add the chickpeas, mixing well.
- Cook for just long enough to heat it all through. The oil from the sausage will turn it all a red colour.
- Remove from the heat and stir in the parsley.
- Serve with crusty bread.

SUMMER PORK WITH SHERRY

MEAT
FAIRLY EASY

This should serve four but it depends on the size of the pork fillets, and how hungry your diners are.

Ingredients

6 - 8 thin pork fillets

2 onions

3 carrots

2 bay leaves

¼ ltr (8 fl oz) Fino de Jerez or similar dry sherry

Salt

Pepper

Olive oil

Method

- Peel the onions and carrots and chop into small pieces.
- Sprinkle a little salt and pepper over the pork. Then, in a large frying pan, heat a little olive oil and brown off the pork fillets on either side. Remove the pork from the pan and set aside.
- In the same oil as the pork, gently fry the onions and carrots until soft, don't allow them to go brown.
- Return the pork to the pan, adding the bay leaves, sherry, salt and pepper.
- Cover and cook gently for about 40 minutes, adding water if necessary, until the pork is tender and the sauce has reduced.
- Serve with creamy mashed potato, rice or a jacket potato.

❝ *August was an awesome month. Minute by minute the sun grew fiercer, forcing folk to take cover in the coolness of their houses. Until evening, the streets stayed deserted and silent except for the panting of dogs under cars. The mountain ranges, once so lush, now reclined, hot, dry and yellow, like lions resting in the midday sun. The olive trees stood bowed, silvery leaves shimmering listlessly in the heat haze.* ❞

From *Chickens, Mules and Two Old Fools*

CREAMY PORK AND PAPRIKA
Cerdo y Pimentón

MEAT
FAIRLY EASY

We love this creamy Spanish pork recipe which is great for an easy dinner or supper, and the smoked paprika adds a lovely hint of Andalucía. When the Gin Twins came for a visit, they cooked it for us.

Ingredients (serves 4)

450g (1lb) boneless pork cut into strips
1 onion, finely chopped
3 cloves garlic, crushed
150g (5 oz) mushrooms, sliced
1 medium green pepper, sliced
Olive oil
1tsp smoked sweet paprika
200ml (7 fl oz) single cream
Small glass of brandy
Bunch fresh parsley, chopped
Salt and pepper

Method

- Season the pork strips with salt, pepper and paprika and set aside on a plate.
- Heat a little olive oil in a deep frying pan and add the onion, cooking until soft.
- Add the mushrooms, pepper and garlic and cook for a few more minutes until the mushrooms are soft. Place the vegetables onto a plate and keep warm.
- Add the pork to the pan and cook on high for a few minutes until browned all over then return the vegetables to the pan. Lower the heat and cook for 15 minutes or so until the pork is cooked through.
- Turn up the heat and add the brandy, cooking on high until almost all has been reduced, then add the cream.
- Lower the heat again and simmer gently for 5 minutes or so until the sauce has thickened.
- Serve with the parsley garnish and an extra sprinkle of paprika, with rice.

" So we sat and watched the level on the brandy bottle descend. I noticed Geronimo's power of speech declined in exact proportion with the amount of brandy left in the bottle. "

From *Chickens, Mules and Two Old Fools*

PACO'S RABBIT STEW
Conejo con Verduras

MEAT — FAIRLY EASY

Rabbit is rarely eaten by some of us nowadays, but this traditional rabbit stew with brandy is often enjoyed by the Spanish and frequently cooked on an open fire.

Ingredients (serves 6)

1 rabbit (prepared and cut into pieces by your friendly butcher or supermarket)

2 onions

2 aubergines (eggplants)

2 red peppers

3 green peppers

6 ripe tomatoes

4 tablespoons olive oil

1 bulb garlic

Medium glass of brandy

Salt and pepper

Method

- Finely chop all the vegetables and set aside.
- Separate the garlic into cloves.
- Heat the oil in a large shallow pan and add the garlic.
- Fry slowly for 5 minutes, then add the rabbit pieces.
- Cook the rabbit slowly for 10 minutes until sealed and slightly golden.
- Add the brandy, cover the pan and continue cooking slowly for a further 20 minutes.
- Remove from the heat and set aside.
- In another pan, heat a little more oil and add the onion, frying until soft.
- Add the aubergines, peppers and brandy juice and cook for about 10 minutes.
- Add the tomatoes. Simmer gently for about an hour, stirring occasionally. The liquid will reduce and become rich and thick.
- Add the rabbit and garlic to the pan, mixing well.
- Season to taste, cover and continue cooking for 20 minutes.
- Serve hot with crusty bread.

> *The usually neat little house was a disaster zone. Rabbit entrails caked the floor and table. Dirty plates and glasses littered every surface. Ashtrays overflowed. The sink was full of pots and pans. Empty beer and wine bottles stood amongst the ornaments. A trail of mud tracked across the floor. Paco looked sheepish as his wife pointed out every sin he had committed. Finally she shrugged, grabbed the floor mop and set to work. I tiptoed out, but not before Paco had winked at me, his eyes full of mischief.*

From *Chickens, Mules and Two Old Fools*

WARMING WINTER'S BRUNCH
Desayuno

MEAT
EASY

This is a very traditional Andalucían breakfast, typically eaten by farmers, shepherds and workers during the winter months.

Ingredients

5 - 6 cloves garlic

1 red pepper

1 jar white beans (or chickpeas, or baked beans)

3 or 4 sweet or spicy chorizos

Olive oil

Method

- Peel and roughly chop the garlic.
- Remove the top and seeds from the pepper, chop into bite-sized chunks.
- In a large frying pan, heat the olive oil and add the garlic and peppers and fry until slightly coloured.
- Chop up the chorizo also into bite-sized chunks and add to the pan, cook for a few minutes on a high heat.
- Add the beans and then lower the heat, cover and cook gently for 20 mins.
- Serve with thick slices of fresh bread.

> Winter in the mountains takes one by surprise. The air is crisp and clean and icy winds funnel through the valley. In the distance, the sea is electric blue, the horizon clearly defined.
>
> Ripening oranges and lemons are bright daubs of paint on a brown canvas. The swallows deserted months ago. At night the temperature can drop to below freezing and village cats sleep on the rooftops huddled close to working chimneys.
>
> From *Chickens, Mules and Two Old Fools*

CARMEN-BETHINA'S POOR MAN'S POTATOES
Patatas a lo Pobre

VEGETARIAN
FAIRLY EASY

This must be one of Spain's most iconic dishes. The ingredients are cheap, but filling and utterly delicious.

Ingredients (serves 4)

15 tbsp olive oil

1 kg (2lb) potatoes - peeled, cut into chunks

3 large onions

3 green peppers - seeded, roughly chopped

Large handful mushrooms wiped, roughly chopped

5 cloves garlic - roughly chopped

4 fresh bay leaves

Salt and freshly ground black pepper to taste

Method

- Heat 5 tablespoons of oil in a large saucepan.
- Add the onion and pinch of salt.
- Cook slowly on a lowish to medium heat for 20 - 30 minutes, stirring frequently until onion is golden brown and soft.
- Add the peppers, mushrooms, garlic and bay leaves.
- Cook for another 15 minutes.
- Meanwhile, chop the potatoes and salt lightly.
- When the peppers are soft, add the remaining oil.
- Ensure the oil is hot before adding the potato chunks.
- Simmer gently for 20 - 30 minutes, stirring occasionally, until the potatoes are soft.
- Drain using a slotted spoon or colander.
- Serve with fresh crusty bread, or as an accompaniment with roast pork or lamb.

" A delicious meal of patatas a lo pobre (poor man's potatoes) was conjured up and set on the table. The meal was not rushed, but eventually the women cleared away, while the men wheeled out the barrel contraption and set it up with buckets placed under. Next, the first crates of grapes were hauled in. Time to begin work. "

"Veeky, watch me," said Bethina.

From *Chickens, Mules and Two Old Fools*

COLIN'S SPANISH OMELETTE
Tortilla de Patatas

VEGETARIAN
SOME SKILL

(Exactly as Colin dictated, hence the occasional rather, um… surprising word… Nevertheless, delicious.)

Ingredients

8 or 9 eggs

About half a kilo of spuds, peeled and sliced thinly

A generous pinch of salt

50% olive, 50% vegetable oil

possibly some lemon juice

a proper non-stick 20 cm frying pan

a circular dinner plate

45 - 60 minutes

Colin says, "And here's what you do…"

- *Half fill the pan with the oil. Heat it gently. Put the spuds in the oil, and stir to make sure they are all coated. The idea is to soften the spuds without browning them. It'll take about half an hour, and you need to give them a stir every now and again.*

- *When the potatoes are cooked, remove them from the oil. If you don't expect to eat the tortilla all in one go, you can sprinkle lemon juice on them - this'll stop them from going grey over the next few days (nothing wrong with the spuds in your tortilla going grey - it just doesn't look very appetising).*

- *Break your eggs into a bowl, throw in the salt, and beat with a frisk or fork until the egg whites and yolks are thoroughly mixed.*

- *Add the spuds and stir.*

- *Drain most of the oil from the pan, leaving a thin coating. Turn up the heat a little (about 60% of full), and pour the egg and potato mixture in.*

- When the mixture has begun to set, pull the edges away from the pan with a splatula - you're trying to get a rounded shape to the edge of the tortilla.
- Now comes the tricky bit - turning it over which can be pretty clumbersome. The Spanish do it by holding an oiled dinner plate against the top of the pan, and flopping them over. In Spain, you can buy a thing called a vuelca de tortilla, basically a plastic lid with a knob on one side for holding it.
- Once you have the tortilla on the plate, slide it back into the pan and carry on cooking and shaping the edge. Turn it two more times, so each side gets cooked twice, and when you have a nice golden colour on both sides, you're done.
- It's important not to overcook the tortilla. I prefer ones that still have a little bit of runniness in the centre, but more sensitive souls prefer them to be cooked solid.
- Let it cool for a bit, and then cut yourself a wodge and serve with a hank of crunchy baguette and a cafe con leche. Perfect!

> Colin was colour blind as well as clumsy. I had asked for creamy, terracotta coloured slabs to be laid in the garden. When the delivery truck arrived, I nearly had a fit. The slabs were salmon pink. Joe and I watched them being unloaded.
>
> "I never ordered pink slabs! I told Colin I wanted terracotta! I wanted a nice neutral colour!"
>
> "Now, come on, Vicky," said Joe, scratching his nethers thoughtfully. "It doesn't matter. They're not that bad. It's only because they're new that they look so…"
>
> "Awful?"

From *Chickens, Mules and Two Old Fools*

GAZPACHO (COLD TOMATO SOUP)
Gazpacho Andaluz

VEGETARIAN EASY

Hollow out some lengths of cucumber to form 'glasses' to serve this popular Spanish summer starter. Spectacular!

Ingredients (serves 4)

2 or 3 slices of white bread

4 large tomatoes

1 small cucumber peeled

1 clove of garlic (finely chopped)

half a small onion

1 small red pepper

3 tablespoons of olive oil

2 tablespoons of white wine vinegar

salt and pepper to taste

water

ice cubes to serve

Method

- Pull the bread to pieces and soak in a cup of water.
- Roughly chop the tomatoes, pepper, onion and cucumber.
- Place in a food processor and blend to a smooth paste.
- Squeeze the bread to remove excess water, add the oil, vinegar and seasoning.
- Blend for a second time, adding water little by little until you achieve the desired consistency.
- Refrigerate until well chilled.
- Serve in tall glasses with crushed ice, or hollow out cucumber 'glasses'.

> *In the heat of summer, we often escaped for a day on the beach.*
>
> *"The beach?" exclaimed Judith one day. "Mmm, quite fancy that meself! Let me know next time you plan to go, dears. Mother won't come, stays out of the sun, don't you know. But I'll join you."*
>
> *Judith a beach babe? I couldn't quite picture that. And I knew with absolute certainty that a day on the beach with Judith would be eventful.*

From *Chickens, Mules and Two Old Fools*

ROAST PUMPKIN WITH CHILI AND HONEY

VEGETARIAN
EASY

This recipe for roast pumpkin combines the flavour of chili pepper with honey. A great vegetarian side dish or to accompany main meals. Butternut squash can be used instead of pumpkin.

Ingredients

1kg (2.25 lb) pumpkin
4 small onions
Pinch of chili flakes
4 tablespoons of honey
100ml (3.4 fl oz) wine vinegar
Olive oil
Salt

Method

- Cut the pumpkin into good-sized wedges, leaving the skin on.
- Quarter the onions and arrange on a baking tray with the pumpkin.
- Drizzle with olive oil, scatter over with the chili flakes and lightly season with salt. Bake for 40 minutes.
- 5 minutes before the pumpkin is ready, heat the wine vinegar and the honey in a pan and bring to the boil, then let simmer for 5 minutes.
- Serve the roasted pumpkin with a generous drizzle of the honey mixture.

The kitchen was as hot as Hades and suffused with a million different cooking aromas.
Bianca, their over-fed spaniel, sat panting under the kitchen table, poised to gobble up any scrap that was thrown in her direction.

From *Two Old Fools - Olé!*

TEPSI
Aubergine, Onion and Potato Bake

VEGETARIAN
FAIRLY EASY

Nadia says, "This dish fills the house with such a delicious aroma that guests are instantly soothed the moment you open your front door."

Top Tips: Sprinkling salt over the aubergines draws out the bitterness. It also means they absorb less oil during the frying stage. Also, remember if your oil is not sufficiently hot, you may end with very greasy aubergines.

Ingredients (serves 4)

2 aubergines, thickly sliced

Salt and black pepper

2 large potatoes, peeled

2 large tomatoes

2 large onions, peeled

4 garlic cloves, peeled

Olive oil

Vegetable oil

200ml (7 fl oz) lamb or vegetable stock

Juice of ½ a lemon

1 tbsp tomato purée

2 - 3 tsp ground mixed spice (or pumpkin pie spice if in the US)

Method

- Preheat the oven to 180°C/gas mark 4.
- Place the sliced aubergines in a colander. Sprinkle salt all over them and leave aside for an hour.
- Slice the potatoes, tomatoes and onions, to the same thickness as the aubergines.
- Thinly slice the garlic.
- Pour 2 - 3 glugs (maybe more) olive oil into a frying pan. Gently fry the onions and garlic until they just begin to brown. Remove the onions and garlic with a slotted spoon and set aside.
- Add a splash of vegetable oil to the olive oil and bring slowly up to heat.
- Fry the potatoes slowly until they are golden brown and almost cooked through. Remove the potatoes and set aside.
- Rinse the salt off the aubergines and thoroughly dry them with kitchen paper.
- Add a bit more vegetable oil and bring slowly up to heat. Gently fry the aubergines until they are golden brown.
- Place on kitchen paper to remove excess oil.
- In a baking dish, alternately layer the aubergine, tomato, onion and garlic, and potato, sprinkling each layer with spice, salt and pepper.
- Pour the stock, lemon juice and tomato purée into the dish, and bake uncovered for 50-60 minutes.

LENTILS AND OYSTER MUSHROOMS

VEGETARIAN EASY

Lentils are very popular in Andalucía and this recipe is for a delicious (and warming) winter snack or light lunch.

Ingredients (serves 3)

500g (17½ oz) oyster mushrooms, sliced
2 cups Spanish lentils, washed
4 cloves of garlic, sliced thinly
12 cherry tomatoes, halved
1 small onion, diced
1 teaspoon hot smoked paprika
Amoroso sherry
Broadleaf parsley (handful, roughly chopped)
Cracked black pepper
Olive oil
Salt
1 litre (33.8 US fl.oz) water

Method

- Sauté the onions and garlic in a splash of olive oil.
- Add the lentils and water. Bring to the boil.
- Leave to simmer until the ingredients are tender.
- Add the hot smoked paprika, season with salt, and pour in about 100ml (3½ US fl.oz) of sherry.
- Meanwhile, fry the oyster mushrooms in a hot frying pan.
- When cooked, add the halved cherry tomatoes, a splash of sherry, and season with salt and pepper.
- Divide the lentils into bowls and arrange the oyster mushrooms and tomatoes over the top.
- Season again with a little cracked black pepper and lightly dust with smoked paprika.

> *Walls that had withstood hundreds of years of blistering summers and freezing winters gave up their fight and were reduced to a pile of rubble. One day, the derelict house next to old Marcia's shop surrendered and collapsed into a mound of debris.*
>
> From *Two Old Fools - Olé!*

HONEY, FIGS AND HAM

MEAT
EASY

When Facebook friend, Linda Hawkswell, showed us all what she was having for lunch, everybody drooled. What a delicious, refreshing, simple, summer lunch or starter! No cooking and ready in minutes. It definitely deserves a place in this cookbook!

Ingredients (serves 2 as a starter)

12 black figs
Runny honey
A few slices of serrano ham
Ground mixed peppercorns

Method

- Wash and quarter the figs.
- Douse the figs liberally in honey and
- dust lightly with ground mixed peppercorns.
- Toss to ensure the figs are coated.
- Place bite-sized pieces of serrano ham over the top.

Black figs freshly picked from our tree this morning and local Andalucian honey. I could eat this every day!

Linda Hawkswell, Facebook friend, reader and fig fan.

TRUE FALAFELS

**VEGETARIAN
SOME SKILL**

"Whatever you do, don't ignore this recipe!" says Nadia. "If there's only one recipe you do in this book, do this one!"

I agree with Nadia; true falafels, unlike the horrid versions from supermarkets, have to be gloriously spicy. They must have a crispy-on-the-outside crunch with a light-and-fluffy-on-the-inside bit-of-give.

Ingredients (serves 4 - 6)

175g (6 oz) dried chickpeas, pre-soaked in cold water for 24 hrs

85g (3 oz) dried fava beans, pre-soaked in cold water for 24 hrs

A handful of fresh parsley

A handful of coriander leaves

2 tsp of ground cinnamon

2 tsp of ground cumin

2 tsp of ground coriander

1 tsp ground allspice

1½ tsp each of salt

1½ tsp freshly ground black pepper

1 tsp cayenne pepper (optional)

2 garlic cloves, peeled

¼ green pepper, seeded and very finely chopped.

2 tbsp flour

3 tbsp sesame seeds

Groundnut oil (for deep frying)

1 tsp bicarbonate of soda (providing lightness to the falafels)

Method

- Drain the chickpeas and fava beans.
- Chop the parsley and coriander, then whizz in a blender until fine. Add the chickpeas, fava beans, spices, garlic, baking soda, green pepper and flour.
- Blend until it is a smooth paste.
- Stir in the sesame seeds and leave to rest for about an hour in the fridge.
- Gently heat the groundnut oil in a deep-fat frying pan. (Test for heat by dropping a small amount of the mixture into the oil - if it sizzles, it's ready.)
- Gently add 1 tbsp of the mixture at a time, as many as possible, without overcrowding them.
- Wait till they float to the top, then gently turn them over. Fry for a couple of minutes until they are golden brown.
- Drain on kitchen paper.
- Serve with pita bread, tahini sauce and pickles.

MEJEDDARAH
A Humble Rice and Lentil Pleasure

VEGETARIAN
SOME SKILL

"Mejeddarah is a humble pleasure of a dish, consisting of fragrant basmati rice, brown lentils and masses of fried onions gently spiced with cumin and black pepper. In our family, we serve it with a chunky tomato and cucumber salad and thick, creamy yoghurt," writes Nadia. "It's really important for this dish that you have a good heavy-bottomed pan with a tightly fitting lid, otherwise the rice and lentils will burn and there will be no saving them!"

Ingredients (serves 4)

125g (4½ oz) brown lentils, washed

2 onions, peeled and chopped

4 onions, peeled and sliced

1 tsp each of ground cumin and ground cinnamon

Plenty of salt and black pepper

6 - 7 tbsp olive oil.

150g (5½ oz) basmati rice

A pinch of granulated sugar

Method

- Place the lentils in 250 ml (9 fl oz) of water, bring to the boil, then turn down the heat.
- Cook until almost tender and the water has been absorbed: about 20 - 30 minutes. Add more water if they begin to dry out.
- Meanwhile, gently fry the chopped onions and spices, with ½ tsp black pepper, in 2 tbsp olive oil.
- When the onions are a deep golden brown, mix with the rice and add some salt and pepper.
- Add the rice and onion mixture to the cooked lentils, adding water until it is 1cm (½ inch) above the top of the rice. Check the seasoning, then cover with a tight-fitting lid.
- Cook on a very low heat for about 15 minutes, until small holes appear in the rice surface.
- Meanwhile, in a large frying pan, Heat 4 - 5 tbsp olive oil.
- Fry the sliced onions for a few minutes, then reduce the heat a little.
- Sprinkle the onions with sugar and cook until they are dark brown.
- Turn the rice and lentils into a bowl and top with the fried onions.

LENTIL DREAM

VEGETARIAN
SOME SKILL

In Nadia's words, "This dish is a dream, not only because of its gorgeous flavours but also because it's a dream come true for any host who has both veggie and non-veggie guests. It's a fantastic accompaniment for lamb, chicken or fish, but also works well with just rice and salad."

Ingredients (serves 2, or 6 - 8 as a side dish)

170g (6 oz) brown lentils

4 tbsp olive oil

4 onions peeled and sliced

1 whole garlic bulb, peeled and crushed

A very large bunch of fresh coriander, chopped

1 tsp fine salt

1 heaped tsp each of ground cumin and ground allspice

1tbs lemon juice, or to taste

1 tsp pomegranate syrup (from Middle Eastern/Turkish shops, large supermarkets or online)

Method

- In a heavy-based saucepan, simmer the lentils in 750ml (1¼ pints) water for 20 minutes.
- Remove from the heat, drain, and set aside.
- Heat 2 tbsp of the oil in a frying pan and fry the onions until they are brown.
- Remove the onions with a slotted spoon and set aside.
- In the same pan, heat the remaining 2 tbsp of oil, then add the garlic. Cook for 1 - 2 minutes stirring continuously.
- Add the coriander and stir until it softens.
- Add half this mixture and half the onions to the lentils. To this lentil mixture, add salt, spices, lemon juice and pomegranate syrup and simmer for 20 minutes.
- Before serving, sprinkle the remaining coriander and onions over the top.

STUFF YA POTATOES

VEGETARIAN
SOME SKILL

Nadia says, "They're delicious, especially with buttered cabbage and onions sitting prettily alongside them."

Ingredients (serves 2 big eaters)

8 potatoes, peeled (Maris Piper are good)

Sunflower oil

Butter

Olive oil

2 tbsp chopped fresh coriander or parsley

For the filling:

4 tbsp pine nuts

1 medium onion, peeled and chopped

1 tsp ground cinnamon

2-3 tsp ground allspice

225g (8 oz) organic minced lamb (not lean - fat adds flavour)

2 tomatoes, finely chopped

Salt and black pepper

3 tbsp tomato purée

300ml (½ pint) lamb stock, hot

Method

- Preheat the oven to 180°C/gas mark 4/350°F.
- Cut off the top of each potato. Core each potato leaving a 1cm (½ inch) shell.
- Fry the potatoes in a little sunflower oil, and a knob of butter, until they are golden brown, then set them aside.
- Heat some sunflower oil in a heavy-based pan.
- Fry the pine nuts until coloured, then set them aside.
- In the same pan, fry the onion until soft, adding more oil if necessary.
- Now add the spices and fry until their aroma is released.
- Stir in the lamb, tomatoes and pine nuts and season well.
- Fill the potatoes with the lamb mixture, leaving a 1cm (½ inch) gap at the top. Lay them side by side in an oven dish.
- Mix the tomato purée with the hot lamb stock.
- Pour around the potatoes until they are halfway covered. Add hot water if necessary.
- Cover with foil and bake for 45 - 50 mins or until tender. For the last 15 minutes, remove the foil and drizzle with olive oil.
- Serve sprinkled with coriander or parsley.

SECTION 3
DRINKS AND DESSERTS

PACO'S SANGRIA
Sangria de Paco

EASY

Sangria is enjoyed all year round, but is particularly pleasant in the hot summer months. Also, there are many fruits in season to choose from. There are hundreds of different sangria recipes in existence, including ones using white wine instead of red. The one rule seems to be: the better the wine, the better the sangria.

Ingredients (serves 4 - 6, maybe)

1 bottle of medium to good quality red wine - chilled

Half teacup sugar

1 can of fizzy lemon drink

1 can of fizzy orange drink

Fruit cut in wedges, not peeled - choose from apples, kiwis, oranges, melon or peaches

Ice cubes

Method

- Pour the wine into a large jug.
- Stir in the sugar with a wooden spoon.
- Add the fizzy drinks, fruit and ice cubes.
- Stir well and serve.

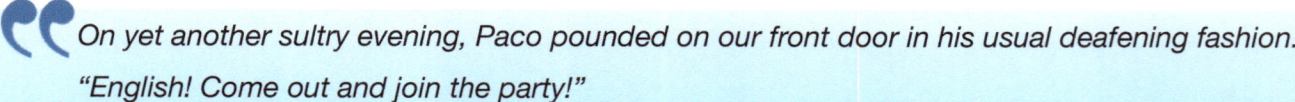

❝ On yet another sultry evening, Paco pounded on our front door in his usual deafening fashion. "English! Come out and join the party!"

To our surprise, the street was full of people. A long table laden down with food had been set up outside our front door, stretching down past Paco's. In the centre was a cake with candles. The table occupied the whole space of the narrow street. Any vehicle rounding the corner would have to stop, reverse and find another way. People could barely squeeze past. ❞

From *Chickens, Mules and Two Old Fools*

THE WINNING RICE PUDDING RECIPE
Arroz con Leche

FAIRLY EASY

Spain is well known for its delicious, fragrant rice pudding, and this traditional recipe won the fiesta contest.

Ingredients

½ kilo (18 oz) white short grain rice

1½ ltr (2½ pints) milk

300ml (11 fl oz) water

100g (3½ oz) sugar

1 small cinnamon stick

Some lemon peel shavings

Pinch salt

Ground cinnamon for dusting

Method

- Place the water, cinnamon stick, lemon peel, salt, sugar and rice in a large pan and bring to the boil.
- Cover and cook on a low heat until most of the water has been absorbed.
- Remove the lemon peel and cinnamon and transfer to an oven proof dish.
- Add the milk and cook in a medium oven for around 20 minutes until the rice is really tender and the dessert is rich and creamy.
- Sprinkle generously with cinnamon.

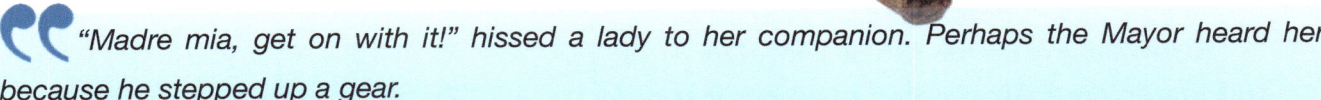

"*Madre mia, get on with it!*" hissed a lady to her companion. Perhaps the Mayor heard her because he stepped up a gear.

"And now the moment has arrived," he announced. "The decision is made. And so, without further ado…" He paused for effect, enjoying the suspense he was creating. The crowd stopped fidgeting and waited with bated breath.

"The winning dessert this year is… The traditional Andalucían rice pudding in the green ceramic bowl!"

From *Chickens, Mules and Two Old Fools*

STICKY TOFFEE PUDDING a la GLENNYS

FAIRLY EASY

This is the recipe from our home-exchange couple, Glennys and Ken, who won the Pudding Contest at our village fiesta one year.

Ingredients

Pudding

1¼ cups chopped dates
1¼ cups water
1 teaspoon bicarbonate of soda
60g (2 oz) butter
¼ cup castor sugar
2 eggs
1 cup self-raising flour

Sauce

200g (8 oz) brown sugar, firmly packed
1 cup fresh cream
20g (1 oz) butter

Glennys, Australian Home Exchanger

> This is the recipe that I used......however I had to improvise in Spain as the ingredients seemed a little different and we needed a larger amount. I added some chocolate powder to the cake mix, and I baked it in a large dish, not a tin, without turning out and over. I just poured some extra sauce over the top and then cooked it for a few extra minutes and served direct from the large dish.

Method

Grease a deep round cake tin. Line the base with paper. Grease both the pan and the paper.

Combine dates and water in a saucepan and bring to the boil. Remove from heat, add bicarbonate of soda and stand 5 mins.

Blend or process until smooth.

Cream butter and sugar in a small bowl with a mixer until combined.

Beat in eggs one at a time.

Fold in the flour, then date mixture.

Bake in moderate oven for about 50 mins or until cooked through.

Allow to cool slightly and then turn onto a rack over an oven tray.

Pour ¼ cup of sauce over the pudding and return to the oven.

Bake uncovered for 5 mins more.

Serve with sauce and whipped cream.

How to make the toffee sauce

Combine sugar, cream and butter in a saucepan and stir over heat without boiling until sugar is dissolved.

Simmer for 3 mins stirring all the time.

 *Hi Joe and Vicky,*

Very glad you love our home and Rob picked you up from the airport ok. He's pretty reliable. Have you met Amy yet? Did she leave the house nice and tidy for you?

Went shopping again - more successful this time. Well armed with the dictionary of course!! Couldn't find a number of things, but maybe they're not available here. Anyway, had a good time and think that we're set up for the next month!!

Having a try of the sticky pudding recipe today to see if it works...if it is a disaster I think I will leave town before the fiesta!!

Glennys, Australian Home Exchanger

From *Chickens, Mules and Two Old Fools*

MAMA UFARTE'S LEMONY SPONGE
Bizcocho

EASY

This is a very quick sponge, with a lovely lemony tang. The Spanish often eat *bizcocho* for breakfast with coffee or hot chocolate. It is also delicious as a dessert served with ice cream.

Ingredients

5 large eggs

150g (6 oz) sugar

150g (6 oz) plain flour

¾ tsp baking powder

Finely grated rind of ½ lemon

Method

- Divide the sugar in half.
- Separate the eggs and beat the whites into one half of the sugar until the mixture is stiff.
- Beat the egg yolks into the other half of sugar, then fold the two halves together.
- Sift the flour and baking powder. Add the lemon and add to the mixture, little by little.
- Place in a lightly greased round baking tin and bake in the middle of a pre-heated oven at 180C (350F) for approximately 20 minutes.

It is a very simple cake to make and the lemon is very subtle. We enjoyed some of the cake for tea. It certainly rises well and is very light.

Sue Franey, chef and photographer of the Old Fools' recipes

❝ The kitchen was a scene of calm domesticity. The fairies were serving Joe and Snap-On with imaginary cake and invisible hot chocolate.

Joe looked up. "Good gracious!" he said. "I didn't realise it was raining."

I gave him one of my Looks. ❞

From *Two Old Fools - Olé!*

COUSIN ELIAS'S EASY-PEASY CARROT CAKE

EASY

Ingredients (makes a 20 cm or 8 inch cake)

115g (4oz) butter, melted
3 eggs, beaten
5 heaped tbsp natural yoghurt
225g (8oz) carrots, peeled and grated
175g (6oz) ground almonds
115g (4oz) soft light-brown sugar
115g (4oz) shelled walnuts, chopped
55g (2oz) desiccated coconut
115g (4oz) stoned dates, chopped
1 tsp ground cinnamon
½ tsp freshly grated nutmeg
1 tsp baking powder

Method

- Preheat the oven to 170°C/gas mark 3/340°F.
- Grease a 20cm (8 inch) round cake tin and line with lightly oiled greaseproof paper.
- Mix together the melted butter and beaten eggs.
- Add the yoghurt, then the carrots and all the remaining dry ingredients. Mix well.
- Pour the mixture into the prepared cake tin.
- Bake for approximately 1 hour.
- Leave to cool in the tin.
- Turn out onto a wire rack to become completely cold.
- Cut a slice (or two) and enjoy!

THREE KINGS CAKE
Roscón de Reyes

SOME SKILL

This delicious cake is eaten with hot chocolate on the night of Epiphany when the Three Kings arrive and leave gifts for children. Whoever finds the Christ Child figure in the cake is crowned and becomes the 'king' or 'queen' of the banquet. Whoever finds the bean has to pay for next year's roscón.

Ingredients

400g (14 oz) flour

3 eggs

100g (3 - 4oz) butter

100g (3 - 4oz) sugar

1 tsp baking powder

¼ litre (half pint) milk

Zest of 1 lemon

Dried mixed peel or jelly sweets for decorating (the jewels)

Salt

To insert just before baking:
A few Christmas figurines and a dried broad bean or similar.

Method

- Pour 4 tbsp of the milk into a glass and stir in the baking powder.
- Add this to a quarter of the flour and mix together until it forms a dough-like consistency.
- Cover with a clean tea towel and set aside until it doubles in size.
- Place the remainder of the flour in a bowl.
- Add the eggs, sugar and a pinch of salt.
- Add the remainder of the milk and zest of the lemon. Mix well.
- Add the butter and continue mixing for a further 2 minutes.
- Add the dough mixture and combine. As soon as a smooth dough has been achieved, cover and set aside for 2 hours.
- Take up the dough again and knead the mixture a little.
- Now shape it into a ring.
- Wrap some little Christmas figures in foil and also a dried broad bean and push them into the dough.
- Place onto a greased baking tray.
- Brush with milk and decorate using the mixed peel. (Figs, quinces cherries can also be used.)

- Brush with milk and decorate using the mixed peel. (Figs, quinces cherries can also be used.)
- Pour 4 tbsp of the milk into a glass and stir in the baking powder.
- Lightly sprinkle with sugar and place in a pre-heated oven (160°C or 320°F) for 15 to 20 mins.
- Cool on a wire rack before slicing.

> ❝ Another highlight of the day is the Roscón de Reyes, that delicious, highly decorated bread-like cake baked to look like a king's crown. We were invited next door for a slice of cake and mug of hot chocolate.
>
> "Lovely cake," said Joe as he munched his way through the slice of Roscón handed to him by Carmen-Bethina. He took another big bite.
>
> Nobody warned Joe. Nobody told Joe to be careful… ❞
>
> From *Two Old Fools - Olé!*

THE FNJ (FIGGY-NUTTY-JAMMY) BRIOCHE

EASY

Nadia says, "This really is one of the most fabulously Arabic answers to the North American classic, the peanut butter and jello sandwich. The fig jam is just divine, whilst the presence of lightly toasted almonds makes it sparkle."

Ingredients (serves 1)

Fig jam

2 slices brioche, lightly toasted

Flaked almonds, toasted

Method

- Simply spread the jam over the toasted brioche and sprinkle with the toasted almonds.

Mmm, naughty!

BAKLAVA
Sent Directly from Heaven

SOME SKILL

"I must warn you that these delightful delicacies are an expensive indulgence that should probably be allowed out once a year," says Nadia. Feel free to experiment with the flower waters.

Ingredients (makes 20 - 25 pastries)

For the filling

350g (12 oz) shelled pistachio nuts, finely chopped

2 tbsp caster sugar

1 tbsp rosewater

1tsp ground cardamom (optional)

For the syrup

300ml (½ pint) water.

450g (1lb) granulated sugar

1 tbsp lemon juice

1 tbsp each of rosewater and orange-flower water

For the pastry

450g (1lb) packet fresh filo pastry

250g (9 oz) unsalted butter, melted

Method

- In a bowl, mix the filling ingredients, cover and set aside.
- Preheat the oven 180°C/gas mark 4/350°F. Butter a 30 x 28 cm (12 x11 inch) baking tray.
- Bring the water, sugar and lemon juice to the boil in a medium saucepan. Don't stir but keep it bubbling for about 4-5 minutes.
- Add the flower waters and set aside to cool.

- Unwrap the pastry and keep under a damp towel or it will very quickly dry out. (Be warned!)
- Lay one sheet in the baking tray and brush it with butter. Repeat, without pressing too hard, until you've used half the pastry packet.
- Now scatter the sugared pistachio mixture all over the pastry.
- Repeat the buttering and layering of the remaining pastry.
- With a sharp knife, cut diamond or square patterns all the way through.
- Bake for 20 minutes, then increase to 220°C/gas mark 7/425°F and cook for 10 - 15 minutes until puffed and golden.
- Pour the syrup on slowly (you may not need it all).
- Serve cold if you can wait that long!

Sue Franey, chef and photographer of the Old Fools' recipes

Feeling very full, you are so right, you couldn't possibly wait for the Baklava to cool...

Rosewater and Pistachio Ice-Cream

SOME SKILL

Nadia Sawalha won the MasterChef final with this delicious recipe and both judges literally swooned. In fact, one judge said he wanted to move next door to her!)

Ingredients (serves 4 - 6)

150ml (5 fl oz) full-fat cream

150ml (5 fl oz) double cream

55g (2oz) shelled ground pistachio nuts

½ tsp very finely ground cardamom seeds (use a pestle and mortar)

2 egg yolks

85g (3oz) caster sugar

2 tbsp rosewater

A drop of red food colouring

Rose petals to decorate (optional)

Method

- Pour the cream, nuts and cardamom into a saucepan. Bring to the boil then set aside.
- Beat the egg yolks and sugar in a bowl until they are pale, then beat in the boiled cream and milk.
- Put it all back into the saucepan and stir constantly over a very low heat. Continue stirring until the consistency is that of custard but never allow it to boil!
- Add the rosewater and food colouring.
- Place all in an ice-cream maker and churn until thick and creamy. (If you don't have one, put the mixture in a plastic container and put in the freezer, stirring every now and then to break up the ice crystals.)
- Scatter the rose petals on top to serve.

The ice cream was amazing. I made double the mix so we had more to indulge in and I used a lovely scented rose from my garden.

Sue Franey, chef and photographer of the Old Fools' recipes

ACKNOWLEDGEMENTS

*Special thanks to **Sue Franey** who used the dark Covid-19 lockdown days to cook countless recipes from this book and photograph each one. Sue, you are amazing, and it was your fabulous photos that inspired me to produce my first all-colour, hardback cookbook in addition to the usual ebook.*

*Also thanks to the village ladies for the Spanish recipes, also **Gayle Macdonald** and her husband, and all the other generous contributors. And thanks to **Nadia Sawalha** and her mum, **Bobbie**, for their Middle Eastern recipes.*

And biggest thanks must go to you for reading the books and joining us in the kitchen.

ABOUT THE AUTHOR

Victoria Twead is the New York Times bestselling author of *Chickens, Mules and Two Old Fools* and the subsequent books in the *Old Fools* series.

After living in a remote mountain village in Spain for eleven years, and owning probably the most dangerous cockerel in Europe, Victoria and Joe retired to Australia.

Another joyous life-chapter has begun.

CONTACTS AND LINKS

Email: TopHen@VictoriaTwead.com (emails welcome)

Website: www.VictoriaTwead.com

Old Fools' Updates newsletter sign-up: www.VictoriaTwead.com

This includes the latest Old Fools' news, free books, book recommendations, and recipe. Guaranteed spam-free and sent out every few months.

Free Stuff: http://www.victoriatwead.com/Free-Stuff/

Facebook: https://www.facebook.com/VictoriaTwead (friend requests welcome)

Instagram: @victoria.twead

Twitter: @VictoriaTwead

THE OLD FOOLS SERIES BY VICTORIA TWEAD
All available in Ebook, Paperback and Large Print editions

Old Fools series, Book 1 (Memoirs)

★ Top 10 Wall Street Journal bestseller ★

Chickens, Mules and Two Old Fools

If Joe and Vicky had known what relocating to a tiny mountain village in Andalucía would REALLY be like, they might have hesitated...

Old Fools series, Book 2

Two Old Fools - Olé!

Vicky and Joe have finished fixing up their house and look forward to peaceful days enjoying their retirement. Then the fish van arrives, and instead of delivering fresh fish, disgorges the Ufarte family.

Old Fools series, Book 3

★ New York Times bestseller three times ★

Two Old Fools on a Camel

Reluctantly, Vicky and Joe leave Spain to work for a year in the Middle East. Incredibly, the Arab revolution erupted, throwing them into violent events that made world headlines.

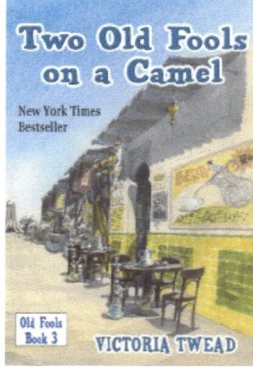

Old Fools series, Book 4

Two Old Fools in Spain Again

Life refuses to stand still in tiny El Hoyo. Lola Ufarte's behaviour surprises nobody, but when a millionaire becomes a neighbour, the village turns into a battleground.

Old Fools series, Book 5

Two Old Fools in Turmoil

When dark, sinister clouds loom, Victoria and Joe find themselves facing life-changing decisions. Happily, silver linings also abound. A fresh new face joins the cast of well-known characters but the return of a bad penny may be more than some can handle.

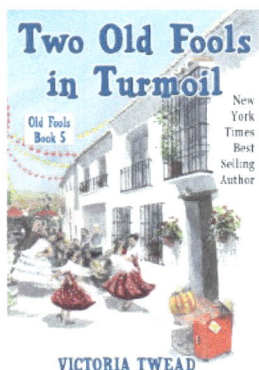

Old Fools series, Book 6

Two Old Fools Down Under

When Vicky and Joe wave goodbye to their beloved Spanish village, they face their future in Australia with some trepidation. Now they must build a new life amongst strangers, snakes and spiders the size of saucers. Accompanied by their enthusiastic new puppy, Lola, adventures abound, both heartwarming and terrifying.

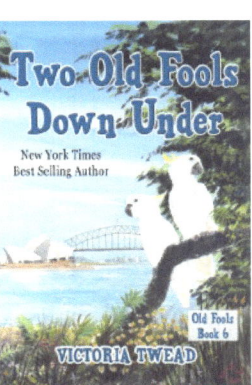

One Young Fool in Dorset (Prequel)

This light and charming story is the delightful prequel to Victoria Twead's Old Fools series. Her childhood memories are vividly portrayed, leaving the reader chuckling and enjoying a warm sense of comfortable nostalgia.

One Young Fool in South Africa (Prequel)

Who is Joe Twead? What happened before Joe met Victoria and they moved to a crazy Spanish mountain village? Joe vividly paints his childhood memories despite constant heckling from Victoria at his elbow

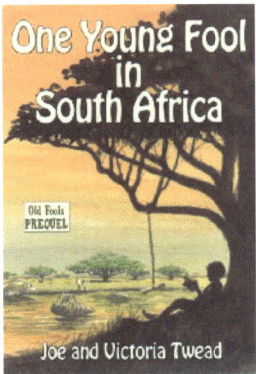

MORE BOOKS BY VICTORIA TWEAD
All available in Ebook, Paperback and Large Print editions

Sixpenny Cross series, Book 1 (Fiction)
A is for Abigail

Abigail Martin has everything: beauty, money, a loving husband, and a fabulous house in the village of Sixpenny Cross. But Abigail is denied the one thing she craves... A baby.

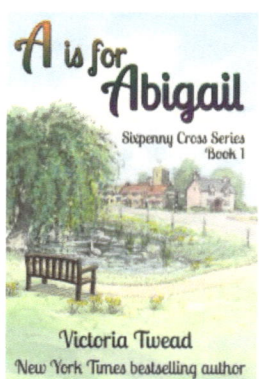

Sixpenny Cross series, Book 2
B is for Bella

When two babies are born within weeks of each other in the village of Sixpenny Cross, one would expect the pair to become friends as they grow up. But nothing could be further from the truth.

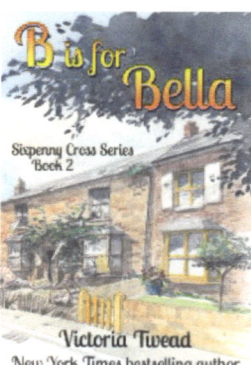

Sixpenny Cross series, Book 3
C is for the Captain

Everyone knows ageing bachelors, the Captain and Sixpence, are inseparable. But when new barmaid, Babs, begins work at the Dew Drop Inn, will she enhance their twilight years, or will the consequences be catastrophic?

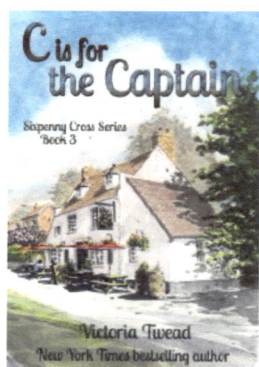

The Sixpenny Cross Collection: Books 1-3

"Wonderfully woven stories set in the delightful village of Sixpenny Cross, with plenty of twists and turns to keep one gripped."

"Another triumph from New York Times bestselling author, Victoria Twead."

"Some authors just have the knack of getting it right, don't they?"

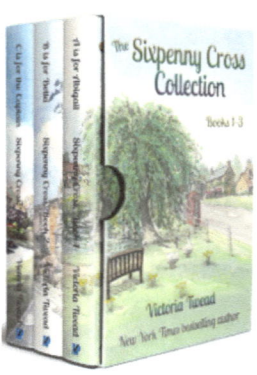

How to Write a Bestselling Memoir

How does one write, publish and promote a memoir? How does one become a bestselling author?

"Victoria Twead opens a window into the world of a bestselling author and shares the insider secrets that helped her get there. *How to Write a Bestselling Memoir* is a must-read not just for memoir writers, but for any author hoping to take their book to the next level." CJ McDaniel - CEO of Adazing.

Morgan and the Martians - A Comedy Play for Kids

Age 7 - 11

Morgan is a bad boy. A VERY bad boy. When a bunch of Martians gives him a Shimmer Suit that makes him invisible, he wastes no time in wearing it to school and creating havoc. Well, wouldn't you?

Two Old Fools in the Kitchen, Part 1 (Cookbook)

Spanish and Middle Eastern Recipes

The *Old Fools' Kitchen* cookbooks were created in response to frequent requests from readers of the *Old Fools series* asking to see all the recipes collected together in one place.

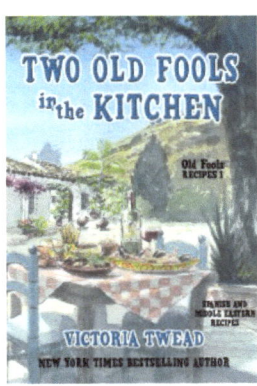

FUTURE BOOKS BY VICTORIA TWEAD

Old Fools series, Book 7
Two Old Fools 7 (working title)

Sixpenny Cross series, Book 4
D is fo Dexter

Two Old Fools in the Kitchen, Part 2 (Cookbook)

Chickens, Mules and Two Old Fools
Book 1 of the Old Fools series
Preview

"Hello?"

"This is Kurt."

"Oh! Hello, Kurt. How are you?"

"I am vell. The papers you vill sign now. I haf made an appointment vith the Notary for you May 23rd, 12 o'clock."

"Right, I'll check the flights and…" but he had already hung up.

Kurt, our German estate agent, was the type of person one obeyed without question. So, on May 23rd, we found ourselves back in Spain, seated round a huge polished table in the Notary's office. Beside us sat our bank manager holding a briefcase stuffed with bank notes.

Nine months earlier, we had never met Kurt. Nine months earlier, Joe and I lived in an ordinary house, in an ordinary Sussex town. Nine months earlier we had ordinary jobs and expected an ordinary future.

Then, one dismal Sunday, I decided to change all that.

"…heavy showers are expected to last through the Bank Holiday weekend and into next week. Temperatures are struggling to reach 14 degrees…"

August, and the weather-girl was wearing a coat, sheltering under an umbrella. June had been wet, July wetter. I sighed, stabbing the 'off' button on the remote control before she could depress me further. Agh! Typical British weather.

My depression changed to frustration. The private thoughts that had been tormenting me so long returned. Why should we put up with it? Why not move? Why not live in my beloved Spain where the sun always shines?

I walked to the window. Raindrops like slug trails trickled down the windowpane. Steely clouds hung low, heavy with more rain, smothering the town. Sodden litter sat drowning in the gutter.

"Joe?" He was dozing, stretched out on the sofa, mouth slightly open. "Joe, I want to talk to you about something."

Poor Joe, my long-suffering husband. His gangly frame was sprawled out, newspaper slipping from his fingers. He was utterly relaxed, blissfully unaware that our lives were about to change course.

How different he looked in scruffy jeans compared with his usual crisp uniform. But to me, whatever he wore, he was always the same, an officer and a gentleman. Nearing retirement from the Forces, I knew he was looking forward to a tension-free future, but the television weather-girl had galvanised me into action. The metaphorical bee in my bonnet would not be stilled. It buzzed and grew until it became a hornet demanding attention.

"Huh? What's the matter?" His words were blurred with sleep, his eyes still closed. Rain beat a tattoo on the window pane.

"Joe? Are you listening?"

"Uhuh…"

"When you retire, I want us to sell up and buy a house in Spain." Deep breath.

There. The bomb was dropped. I had finally admitted my longing. I wanted to abandon England with its ceaseless rain. I wanted to move permanently to Spain.

Sleep forgotten, Joe pulled himself upright, confusion in his blue eyes as he tried to read my expression.

"Vicky, what did you say just then?" he asked, squinting at me.

"I want to go and live in Spain."

"You can't be serious."

"Yes, I am."

Of course it wasn't just the rain. I had plenty of reasons, some vague, some more solid.

I presented my pitch carefully. Our children, adults now, were scattered round the world; Scotland, Australia and London. No grandchildren yet on the horizon and Joe only had a year before he retired. Then we would be free as birds to nest where we pleased.

And the cost of living in Spain would be so much lower. Council tax a fraction of what we usually paid, cheaper food, cheaper houses… The list went on.

Joe listened closely and I watched his reactions. Usually, *he* is the impetuous one, not me. But I was well aware that his retirement fantasy was being threatened. His dream of lounging all day in his dressing-gown, writing his book and diverting himself with the odd mathematical problem was being exploded.

"Hang on, Vicky, I thought we had it all planned? I thought you would do a few days of supply teaching if you wanted, while I start writing my book." Joe absentmindedly scratched his nether regions. For once I ignored his infuriating habit; I was in full flow.

"But imagine writing in Spain! Imagine sitting outside in the shade of a grapevine and writing your masterpiece."

Outside, windscreen wipers slapped as cars swept past, tyres sending up plumes of filthy water.

Joe glanced out of the window at the driving rain and I sensed I had scored an important point.

"Why don't you write one of your famous lists?" he suggested, only half joking.

I am well known for my lists and records. Inheriting the record- keeping gene from my father, I can't help myself. I make a note of the weather every day, the temperature, the first snowdrop, the day the ants fly, the exchange rate of the euro, everything. I make shopping lists, separate ones for each shop. I make To Do lists and 'Joe, will you please' lists. I make packing lists before holidays. I even make lists of lists. My nickname at work was Schindler.

So I set to work and composed what I considered to be a killer pitch:

- Sunny weather
- Cheap houses
- Live in the country
- Ridiculously low council tax
- Friendly people
- Less crime
- No heating bills
- Cheap petrol
- Wonderful Spanish food
- Cheap wine and beer
- Could get satellite TV so you won't miss English football
- Much more laid-back life style
- Could afford house big enough for family and visitors to stay
- No TV licence
- Only short flight to UK
- Might live longer because Mediterranean diet is healthiest in the world

When I ran dry, I handed the list to Joe. He glanced at it and snorted.

"I'm going to make a coffee," he said, but he took my list with him. He was in the kitchen a long time.

When he came out, I looked up at him expectantly. He ignored me, snatched a pen and scribbled on the bottom of the list. Satisfied, he threw it on the table and left the room. I grabbed it and read his additions. He'd pressed so hard with the pen that he'd nearly gone through the paper.

Joe had written:

    CAN'T SPEAK SPANISH!
    TOO MANY FLIES!
    MOVING HOUSE IS THE PITS!

For weeks we debated, bouncing arguments for and against like a game of ping pong. Even when we weren't discussing it, the subject hung in the air between us, almost tangible.

Then, one day (was it a coincidence that it was raining yet again?) Joe surprised me.

"Vicky, why don't you book us a holiday over Christmas, and we could just take a look."

The hug I gave him nearly crushed his ribs.

"Hang on!" he said, detaching himself and holding me at arm's length. "What I'm trying to say is, well, I'm willing to compromise."

"What do you mean, 'compromise'?"

"How about if we look on it as a five year plan? We don't sell this house, just rent it out. Okay, we could move to Spain, but not necessarily for ever. At the end of five years, we can make up our minds whether to come back to England or stay out there. I'm happy to try it for five years. What do you think?"

I turned it over in my mind. Move to Spain, but look on it as a sort of project? Actually, it seemed rather a good idea. In fact, a perfect compromise.

Joe was watching me. "Well? Agreed?"

"Agreed…" It was a victory of sorts. A Five Year Plan. Yes, I saw the sense in that. Anything could happen in five years.

"Well, go on, then. Book a holiday over Christmas and we'll take it from there."

So I logged onto the Internet and booked a two week holiday in Almería.

Why Almería? Well, we already knew the area quite well as this would be our fourth visit. And I considered this part of Andalucía to be perfect. Only two and a half hours flight from London, guaranteed sunshine, friendly people and jaw-dropping views. It ticked all my boxes. Joe agreed cautiously that the area could be ideal.

So the destination was decided, but what type of home in Spain would we want? Our budget was reduced because we weren't going to sell our English house. We'd have to find something cheap.

On previous visits, I'd hated all the houses we'd noticed in the resorts. Mass produced boxes on legoland estates, each identical, each characterless and overlooking the next. No, I knew what I really wanted: a house we could fix up, with views and space, preferably in an unspoiled Spanish village.

Unlike Joe, I've always been obsessed with houses. I was the driving force and it was the hard climb up the English property ladder that allowed us even to contemplate moving abroad. In the past few years, we had bought a derelict house, improved and sold it, making a good profit. So we bought another and repeated the process. It was gruelling work. We both had other careers, but it was well worth the effort. Now we could afford to rent out our home in England and still buy a modest house in Spain.

"If we do decide to move out there," said Joe, "and we buy an old place to do up, it's not going to be like doing up houses in England. Everything's going to be different there."

How right he was.

Chickens, Mules and Two Old Fools and the *Old Fools series* are available from all good book stores and public libraries.

Lightning Source UK Ltd.
Milton Keynes UK
UKHW051613180920
370103UK00003B/46